The
Spiritual
Laws
of Life

Also by Harold Klemp

MAHANTA

The
Spiritual
Laws
of Life

Harold Klemp

ECKANKAR
Minneapolis

Compiled by Mary Carroll Moore

Edited by Joan Klemp and Anthony Moore

Text illustrations by Signy Cohen

Cover photo by Robert Huntley

Publisher's Cataloging-in-Publication
(Provided by Quality Books, Inc.)

Klemp, Harold
    The spiritual laws of life / Harold Klemp.
    p. cm.
    LCCN: 2002107255
    ISBN: 1-57043-176-0

    1. Eckankar (Organization) 2. Spiritual life–
Eckankar (Organization) I. Title.

BP605.E3S65 2002   299'.93
                              QBI02-579

We begin to have experiences with the Light and Sound of God, and thus we develop a greater understanding of the spiritual laws of life. Knowing these laws, we can then make our own life easier.

—Harold Klemp,
The Dream Master,
Mahanta Transcripts, Book 8

Contents

Laws of Charity—The laws that bring Soul a greater capacity to love

Foreword

The teachings of ECK define the nature of Soul.
You are Soul, a particle of God sent into this world to gain spiritual experience.

The goal in ECK is spiritual freedom in this lifetime, after which you become a Co-worker with God, both here and in the next world. Karma and reincarnation are primary beliefs.

Key to the ECK teachings is the Mahanta, the Living ECK Master. He has the special ability to act as both the Inner and Outer Master for ECK students. The prophet of Eckankar, he is given respect but is not worshiped. He teaches the sacred name of God, HU. When sung just a few minutes each day, HU will lift you spiritually into the Light and Sound of God—the ECK (Holy Spirit). This easy spiritual exercise and others will purify you. You are then able to accept the full love of God in this lifetime.

Sri Harold Klemp is the Mahanta, the Living ECK Master today. Author of many books, discourses, and articles, he teaches the ins and outs of the spiritual life. His teachings lift people and help them recognize and understand their own experiences in the Light and Sound of God. Many of his talks are available to you on audio- and videocassette.

This book contains thought-provoking quotations from Sri Harold Klemp and from Paul Twitchell, the modern-day founder of Eckankar. Within these pages are many excellent tools to enliven your personal spiritual study and path to mastership.

To find out more about Harold Klemp and Eckankar, please turn to page 205 in the back of this book.

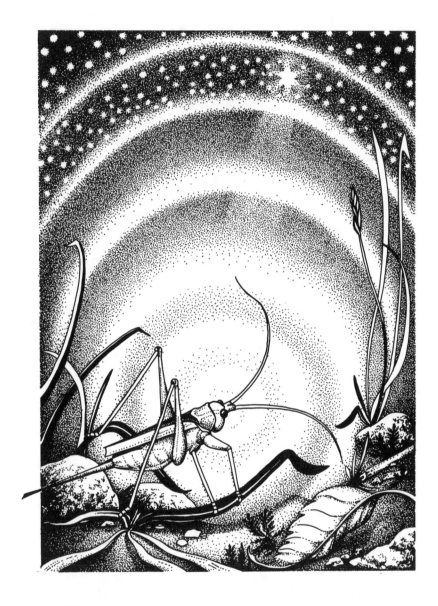

All things from heaven to earth are under Its care; and It hears the faint chirp of the cricket, though It may seem deaf to our loudest prayers.

Laws of Wisdom

The laws that speak of divine power
and how it manifests in the universe

Causation

causation. The wheel of life, which is a factor in the human and spiritual cycles of lives; karma.

A Cosmic Sea of Words: The ECKANKAR Lexicon

The ECK Power is the intelligence which pervades all space and animates all living things; this mental action and reaction is the Law of Causation. The principle of causation does not begin in the individual but in the cosmic power. It is not an objective faculty but a subjective process, and the results are seen in an infinite variety of conditions and experiences.

In order to express life there must be the power. Nothing can exist without the cosmic power. Everything which exists is some manifestation of this basic power from which and by which all things have been created and continually are being recreated.

Man lives in a fathomless sea of this plastic ether called the ECK Power; and this substance is ever alive and active. It is sensitive to the highest degree. Thought form takes mould or matrix from that which the substance expresses.

Dialogues with the Master, **chap. 20**

The other aspect of Spirit, even more important than the Light, is that which we know as the Sound.

The other aspect of Spirit, even more important than the Light, is that which we know as the Sound. This Sound Current is actually the Voice of God, spoken of in the Bible as the Word: "In the beginning was the Word. . . . And the word was made flesh, and dwelt among us." This Voice, the creative current which comes from God, has created the lower worlds. It comes out like a radio wave from a central broadcasting station. It's like a pebble thrown into a quiet lake, causing ripples to go out. These waves go out but they must always come back to the center; it's the returning wave that we are interested in. This is what Soul is looking for: to return to the God center. When It returns to the God center, we call this God-Realization, or the God Consciousness.

This is what Soul is looking for: to return to the God center.

How to Find God, **Mahanta Transcripts, Book 2, chap. 10**

Someone wrote to me from a farm in Africa. He said a hen laid a bunch of eggs that were fertilized by a funny-looking rooster whose head and neck were bald. Every time the rooster would come in the yard, the family would all laugh at it.

It was all pretty funny until the eggs hatched. One of the chicks came out looking exactly like the rooster—bald head, bald neck. Because the little thing was so ugly and small, the other chicks picked on it and finally even broke its leg. To protect it, the family had to bring it into the house.

The person who wrote the letter said, "You know, it's interesting how we laughed at this rooster that was bald-headed and bald-necked, and now all of a sudden we find that one just like him has taken up residence in our home!"

Thoughts of any nature are going to come home to roost. This is called the Law of Karma, or the Law of Cause and Effect. The ECKists are quite familiar with it.

How to Find God, **Mahanta Transcripts, Book 2, chap. 19**

Change

Change, Law of. Conditions in the worlds of time and space will always change at some point; there is no stability here.

A Cosmic Sea of Words: The ECKANKAR Lexicon

This is a world of change. In fact, even this universe plus so many heavens that lie above this physical one are in a constant swirl of change. Change is the unchanging law for the worlds of change.

Wisdom of the Heart, Book 2, **Wisdom Note 28**

Whoever is under the hand of moha is unconscious of the Law of Change, which permeates all things in the lower worlds. There is no stability here, as the positive and negative streams are in a constant interplay that can feature the good things in life for a while, but then can take a discouraging turn toward the unhappy lessons; this dynamic tension between the positive and negative forces is needed to stretch the individual beyond his present capacity.

Soul Travel 2, **lesson 4**

Conditions in this unstable realm of time and space will always change at some point.

Conditions in this unstable realm of time and space will always change at some point. It is one of the laws of these elastic worlds.

The ECK Satsang Discourses, **Fourth Series, lesson 10**

In the chela's rendezvous with destiny, the Mahanta wants to show him the meaning of a single fact: All change is a measure of spiritual growth, and without change there is no growth at all.

The ECK Satsang Discourses, **Third Series, lesson 11**

When people don't understand that a change is for their own good, they usually shut the door to the blessings of God—just because it is change.

Our Spiritual Wake-Up Calls, **Mahanta Transcripts, Book 15, chap. 6**

To be able to accept the changes as you move from the present to the future, or from one plane to another in the present, requires a very nimble state of consciousness.

The Drumbeat of Time, **Mahanta Transcripts, Book 10, chap. 2**

Lightly place your attention upon a situation in your life, then put your viewpoint as Soul above the situation. Look down on everything going on below as if it were a chess game—even though it might be in your imagination. You can look at a situation anywhere in the world from this viewpoint.

As you are gazing upon it, change the situation by simply rearranging your place on the chessboard. It's a successful device, and those who use it often make great changes around themselves.

The Art of Spiritual Dreaming, **chap. 9**

Change is the law of truth here. It sweeps cobwebs from the eye of Soul, showing the right way to a more happy, fruitful life. And yet, despite all the spiritual riches of ECK, chelas forget about them. Odd, isn't it, how human nature selects a small handful of events from the past and makes of them our memories, though it often leaves out the blessings of ECK? Human nature is a fickle child.

Everything in life is about change. Yet it is mostly your ability to change your consciousness to the needs of the moment that counts above all. Graceful change of that sort will keep you spiritually young for all time.

It is mostly your ability to change your consciousness to the needs of the moment that counts above all.

**Wisdom from the Master on Spiritual Leadership:
ECK Leader's Guide, article 42**

As harsh as change may often appear to us, it is for the purification of immature and mature Souls alike.

**Wisdom from the Master on Spiritual Leadership:
ECK Leader's Guide, article 82**

Consciousness

Consciousness, Law of. The recognition, or realization, of the beingness of self or thing in thought, which manifests external life and form.

A Cosmic Sea of Words: The ECKANKAR Lexicon

We each choose our own state of consciousness. It takes a while for many individuals, even many ECK initiates, to recognize this. We make our own worlds. What we are today is the sum total of everything we have thought or been throughout the ages.

How to Find God, **Mahanta Transcripts, Book 2, chap. 1**

Everything in the universe has its origin in idea, in thought, and it has its completion in the manifestation of thought through form. Many intermediate stages are necessary, but the cause and effect of the series are the thought and the thing. This shows that in essence the thing already existed in thought. . . . This is consciousness. If it is a true fact that the thing must be in thought before thought can form the thing, then it is plain that the Divine ideal can only be externalized in our objective life to the proportion it is first formed in our thought. It takes form from our thought only to the extent we have apprehended its existence in the divine ECK. . . .

Soul is the thinker of thoughts. The consciousness responds when directed by Soul, which is beyond all thought, beyond all matter, energy, space, and time. The very act of thinking imposes self-consciousness because all thoughts are possible only through self-consciousness. Therefore, that which I am, that which is above and beyond all thoughts, cannot be revealed by the consciousness nor the intellect. Even when the consciousness cannot think of it, it is possible for Soul, which I am, to know the whole thing in a complete way. . . .

In the creative process of Soul we become the individual reflection of what we realize the divine power to be, relative to one's self. If we realize the divine as the infinite potential of all that can constitute a perfect human being, this conception must, by the law of creativity, gradually build up a corresponding image in our thoughts, which in turn, will act on our external condition.

This, by the Law of Consciousness, is the nature of the process.

The Flute of God, chap. 9

It is one thing to be born into a certain state of consciousness, but we owe it to ourselves to make the effort to reach higher and beyond.

All paths to God are provided by Spirit for the express purpose of giving Soul in Its varying states of consciousness a choice in how It wants to return to God. Each path leads to another path, and then to another. It is one thing to be born into a certain state of consciousness, but we owe it to ourselves to make the effort to reach higher and beyond. Upon birth, we are given whatever consciousness we need to get from birth to death; the kind that allows us to go to school, learn a trade or a profession, and make our way. But it takes a special effort to go beyond and reach greater states of consciousness. We can do this by direct experience with the Light and Sound of Spirit.

How to Find God, **Mahanta Transcripts, Book 2, chap. 8**

Every time you move into another state of consciousness, your nutritional laws may change. Then you start juggling your diet and vitamins. When you finally lose track, you may end up going to a nutritionist. Why? Because you are going through different states of consciousness and your body is responding to the law, As above, so below. As you grow in your state of consciousness or as you come nearer to another initiation, things begin to change and you wonder what's happening. It's simply that your state of consciousness is changing. Even your word, your secret word, may not work anymore, and you must ask to find a new one.

How to Find God, Mahanta Transcripts,
Book 2, chap. 14

It is known in the spiritual order that the expansion of consciousness can only take place after one is put into new conditions of learning.

The ECK Satsang Discourses, **Fourth Series, lesson 9**

Life carries all people and beings onward to the expansion of consciousness.

The Art of Spiritual Dreaming, **chap. 12**

Consciousness is the ECK, but not God Itself. The moment the chela has a consciousness of himself as the ECK, he has established himself in the Word, the Voice of God. This is the realization of Soul that occurs on the Fifth Plane. This leads into God-Realization, the ultimate goal of all chelas who follow the path of ECK.

The Shariyat-Ki-Sugmad, **Book One, chap. 8**

The simplest key to being "conscious" is the art of listening. By all means listen to others, but also

Life carries all people and beings onward to the expansion of consciousness.

listen—and watch—for the silent voice of the Mahanta that speaks through others, the waking dream, and intuition, for example.

To be conscious is to be humble and compassionate in the presence of life. In short, love fills your being. The ego is out.

Wisdom from the Master on Spiritual Leadership: ECK Leader's Guide, article 83

Five Spiritual Laws
of This World

Five Spiritual Laws of This World.   These are just five of the many spiritual laws of this world. They are important especially when looking at political and religious fields. (1) The beginning of human life is when breath comes into the fetus. (2) Love is the first and great commandment; also called the rule of spiritual law: love God, love your neighbor, and love yourself. (3) Work for your food. This deals with the welfare system and our responsibility to make our own way as much as we can in this world. (4) Give tribute to God and Caesar. This relates to our duty to the government regarding taxes. (5) Reward the laborer. This is about the government's duty to the people.

A Cosmic Sea of Words: The ECKANKAR Lexicon

The first law deals with the beginning of human life. The beginning of human life is when breath comes into the fetus. . . .

The backup for this in the Christian Bible is Genesis 2:7. "And the Lord God formed man of the dust of the ground and breathed into his nostrils the breath of life; and man became a living soul." The key point is "and breathed into his nostrils the breath of life."

The Secret of Love, **Mahanta Transcripts, Book 14, chap. 7**

Love is the first and great commandment.

Law number two is: Love is the first and great commandment. . . .

13

This law can also be called the rule of spiritual law. In Matthew 22:37–39, Jesus said, "Thou shalt love the Lord thy God with all thy heart, and with all thy soul, and with all thy mind. This is the first and great commandment. And the second is like unto it, Thou shalt love thy neighbour as thyself."

If the leaders and the people in a society would take these two laws to heart, this would be an entirely different place.

The Secret of Love, **Mahanta Transcripts,**
Book 14, chap. 7

The third law deals with the welfare system. It tells about the responsibility we have to make our own way as much as we can in this world. . . .

Law number three is: Work for your food.

Law number three is: Work for your food.

This comes from Paul in his second letter to the Thessalonians. I am quoting from the King James Version. . . .

"Neither did we eat any man's bread for nought" means that we didn't just take somebody else's bread without doing something in return. "But wrought with labour and travail night and day." We worked and did whatever we could, we did whatever our mission was. . . . But they did all this work night and day "that we might not be chargeable to any of you." Which basically means that we didn't owe you anything in the way of rent or anything else. Nobody could say, "You didn't carry your own weight." Paul was saying, We carried our own weight, and this is the tradition that we were trying to give to the rest of you. These are good principles.

We're addressing the welfare system. Paul continues, "Not because we have not power, but to make ourselves an ensample unto you to follow us." In other words, he was saying, We could be the big guys and say, "We're in town. Take care of us. We're going to do our preaching. Feed us; give us room and board." We could have pulled rank on you, and you would have to put up with it. But we didn't do that. We wanted to be an example for you.

Then he says, "For even when we were with you, this we commanded you." And this is the important point. The people who are putting together legislation for the reform of the welfare system need to understand this: "That if any would not work, neither should he eat." Very simple, very straightforward.

Then he closes: "For we hear that there are some which walk among you disorderly, working not at all, but are busybodies" (2 Thessalonians 3:6–11).

The Secret of Love, **Mahanta Transcripts, Book 14, chap. 7**

Law number four deals with our duty to the government regarding tax levies. Law number four: Give tribute to God and Caesar.

Law number four: Give tribute to God and Caesar.

The Pharisees were trying to trick Jesus into making statements against the Roman government. If they could do this, they could bring the Roman government down on him and have him put in jail. So someone asked him, "Is it lawful to give tribute unto Caesar, or not?"

Jesus was very sharp. "Show me a coin."

They said, "Sure."

They gave him a coin, worth maybe twenty cents. "Whose image is on this coin?" he said.

They said, "Caesar's."

And Jesus said, "Render," which means give, "Render therefore unto Caesar the things which are Caesar's; and unto God the things that are God's"

(Matthew 22:17, 21). They marveled at how he had sidestepped their trap.

The Secret of Love, **Mahanta Transcripts, Book 14, chap. 7**

Law number four was about the people's duty to the government. Law number five is about the government's duty to the people.

This is the one that government officials like to forget about. When they forget about it and take more than their due through taxes, they enslave the people they are ruling. If you don't have money in a society, you have no freedom. . . .

Law number five: Reward the laborer.

In 1 Timothy 5:18, Paul says, "Thou shalt not muzzle the ox that treadeth out the corn. And, The labourer is worthy of his reward."

Paul tried to explain the same concept to the Corinthians in another letter. He quotes this law again, "Thou shalt not muzzle the mouth of the ox that treadeth out the corn." . . .

Here's the whole purpose of incentive, of why people work: "that he that ploweth should plow in hope; and that he that thresheth in hope should be partaker of his hope" (1 Corinthians 9:9–10). If you're plowing and somebody demands that you give your entire crop to Caesar, there's no incentive for you to work. That's what they used to do in the Soviet Union. People didn't work, and today there is no Soviet Union. It was a government trying to enslave its people.

The government said, "Don't worry about things. We'll take care of you." And all they did was suppress and make slaves of their people.

Socialism is the same as communism, just not quite as strong—yet. We have to look out for the

Law number five: Reward the laborer.

spiritual freedom involved in these laws that are reflected in the Christian Bible.

The Secret of Love, **Mahanta Transcripts,
Book 14, chap. 7**

Fixidity

Fixidity, Law of.   A law that governs the dominion of the Kal giving the appearance of completeness, spaciousness, and accommodation yet beset
with numberless restrictions not perceived by anyone except the Spiritual Traveler.

A Cosmic Sea of Words: The ECKANKAR Lexicon

ECK is not bound by the Law of Fixidity.

Soul Travel 2, **lesson 2**

The hidden ECK teachings have survived in a
hardened world due to their flexibility. It is said
that Taoism, the ancient philosophy and religion of
China, outlasted Confucianism, the moral and religious system, because the latter reduced everything to fixed rules. ECK and life are flux; Kal and
limitation are fixed states of consciousness that try
to build prison walls around truth.

*The hidden
ECK teachings
have survived
in a hardened
world due
to their
flexibility.*

Soul Travel 2, **lesson 2**

The lackeys of the Kal Niranjan are misguided
in their search for truth because his region of
dominion is under the Law of Fixidity, which gives
the appearance of spaciousness, accommodation,
and completeness, but is set within a bowl of count-
less restrictions not perceived by anyone but the
Spiritual Traveler.

Soul Travel 2, **lesson 2**

God

God, Law of. Everything has its origin in Spirit; divine truth is one and unchanging.

A Cosmic Sea of Words: The ECKANKAR Lexicon

The odyssey of Soul teaches us to cooperate with the laws of God. It takes many lifetimes of bumps and bruises before all the lessons of Godhood sink in. And when they do, we are granted the grace to partake consciously of the highest aspects of sainthood.

The Living Word, **Book 1, chap. 31**

The Law of God states that "Soul has existence because God wills it." Thus, God loves all life so dearly that It allows Soul to exist. If It did not love life, there would be no life-forms in this universe and all would be barren. Time, space, law, chance, matter, primitive energy, and intelligence are only the effects of God's love for life, and only exist to serve Soul in Its journey to find liberation and freedom.

The Soul is not the cause for the law which brings happiness or misery. Not being free, neither does It act as the prime cause that brings about the opposite. As the free Self It has the opportunity to establish Itself as the prime mover for bringing about happiness and letting life be what it should be. It does not establish life but exists because life itself supports Soul as the prime consideration of God's love for every individual Soul within the universe.

The Shariyat-Ki-Sugmad, **Book One, chap. 8**

The Law of God states that "Soul has existence because God wills it."

There was a time before these lower worlds were created when Soul resided in the heavens. It's difficult to conceive of such a thing in heaven as a selfish, or ungrowing, Soul; but interestingly enough, It wouldn't serve anyone or anything except Itself. And so God sent Soul down into the lower worlds which had been created specifically for Its experience. The hardships and troubles, even the happiness and joy—the full spectrum of experience that we know through the five senses and beyond—are for Soul's unfoldment, so that one day It may become a Co-worker with God. This is the only purpose of it all.

How to Find God, **Mahanta Transcripts, Book 2, chap. 14**

The hardships and troubles, even the happiness and joy are for Soul's unfoldment, so that one day It may become a Co-worker with God.

One of the most prevalent misunderstandings is that the Law of God works only for those who have a devout or religious objective. This is a fallacy. It works just as impersonally as any law of physics. It can be used for greed or selfish purposes, as well as noble ones.

The Key to ECKANKAR, **p. 16**

The ECK Master speaks of the Law of God.

This supreme law speaks to the heart, for it tells of the relationship between the Sugmad (God) and Soul. That law is love. It gives each person an answer to the ancient riddle of life: What is my purpose here? Agnostic or simple believer in a traditional God, all Souls are moving into a greater circle of light and understanding.

The Master 4 Discourses, **lesson 12**

Spiritual enlightenment and illumination come as we have contact with this Light and Sound of

God. The ECKist sees the actual Light of God that comes during contemplation. It gives spiritual upliftment and takes away the karma which has been created throughout our past lives and the daily karma from this lifetime.

We can do without the Light but we can't do without the Sound. It is an actual sound that we hear. It may be that of an orchestra; it may be that of a flute. . . .

This is the only way that God can speak to us, through either the Light or the Sound. Whenever we have an experience on the inner and we hear a booming voice, it may be a Master, whether seen or unseen, another being, or an angel of God—but it's not God. The true Voice is what we seek. It gives the wisdom and the truth which surpasses all understanding.

As we begin to get this Light and Sound in our life, it shows in how we conduct our daily affairs. Our daily life is a reflection of what happens inwardly. We may be spiritually successful, but it doesn't necessarily mean we're going to be rich. If we set a goal for a project, we ought to get a grasp of spiritual principles from the experience. These help us succeed in the sense that these experiences take us to the next step in life. What we call success, other people may call failure, because we have a different viewpoint. And because we have this viewpoint, we have happiness and lightness which many other people would dearly love to experience but have never found.

As we begin to get this Light and Sound in our life, it shows in how we conduct our daily affairs.

How to Find God, **Mahanta Transcripts, Book 2, chap. 15**

God, of Itself, runs a straight course and does not take care of the individual, in a sense, yet It has the individual's welfare close to Its heart. All things from heaven to earth are under Its care; and It hears the faint chirp of the cricket, though It may seem deaf to our loudest prayers.

So we are appointed as ECK Gurus to take care of all who come for help. "Lo, you who are weary and burdened come unto me and I will take your burden." Remember that? This is our responsibility in life.

The Living ECK Master, the Godman who is now living in this physical universe, cares for all life. Trust in him.

The Key to ECKANKAR, **p. 15**

The greatest principle of God is the survival of the individual, that is, Soul.

The greatest principle of God is the survival of the individual, that is, Soul. The dynamic principle of existence is survival.

The Key to ECKANKAR, **p. 27**

Let it be known, here and now, that all knowledge and all wisdom are never given to Soul. For the world of God is without beginning and without ending, infinite in all attributes and qualities, and constantly expanding toward greater truth and greater wisdom.

The Key to ECKANKAR, **p. 29**

Our belief about the liberation of Soul is unlike that of Christianity. A Christian may lead just about any kind of life he wants to, as long as he confesses his sins and accepts the atonement of Jesus in the final hour. In truth, the Law of God is not like that. It is much simpler. When we have love, we act with love. Love is the doorway to heaven. It is not power. It is not control. Nor is it anger. Unless love enters the heart, one has yet to find spiritual freedom.

Wisdom of the Heart, **Book 1, Wisdom Note 9**

Most people overlook the ways that the Holy Spirit speaks to us. It's not that the ways are too humble. It's that the people are too proud to listen. Divine Spirit speaks to us through Its creatures and through nature. It shows us how the Law of God can work if we have the spiritual understanding to see it.

Stories to Help You See God in Your Life,
ECK Parables, Book 4, chap. 2

Divine Spirit speaks to us through Its creatures and through nature.

Grace

Grace, Law of. To be in accord with the ways of the Sugmad for making each a divine channel, through working in the area of nonattachment mainly through discipline of the emotions.

A Cosmic Sea of Words: The ECKANKAR Lexicon

We take our steps on the spiritual path; we climb the ladder to God. Jesus said, "Come unto me and be lifted up." What he tried to explain was simply this: The grace of God does not descend upon us. This is something that religions often do not understand. They feel the grace of God comes to us merely because we ask. It does in a way, but first we must earn it. We must make at least some effort before the grace of God comes to us; but when it does, we are lifted up into it.

How to Find God, **Mahanta Transcripts, Book 2, chap. 1**

We must make at least some effort before the grace of God comes to us; but when it does, we are lifted up into it.

You have to undergo the discipline to lift your state of consciousness to an area where these teachers are, where they can help you. In a sense, we are led to believe that the grace of God descends upon us, but actually it's as Jesus spoke of when he told his followers to come unto him and he would lift them up.

How to Find God, **Mahanta Transcripts, Book 2, chap. 4**

Anyone with a sufficient desire for a realization of God can achieve that realization—the grace of

God will guarantee it.

The Key to ECKANKAR, p. 41

The best approach to spiritual unfoldment is to expect the greatest love and blessings from the divine ECK, but then accept whatever comes your way.

The eternal dreamer starts to see himself more clearly, and often he doesn't like what he sees. He can then either resist who he is—or better yet—accept who he is. This is when he can say, "I am what I am, and I will be that with as much grace as I can muster at this time."

The Art of Spiritual Dreaming, chap. 6

Nothing is ever the same as it was.

If life has a single lesson to teach us, it's that. Many lessons and experiences are similar, but no two will ever be exactly alike. The best approach to spiritual unfoldment is to expect the greatest love and blessings from the divine ECK, but then accept whatever comes your way.

Expect, but accept.

Wisdom from the Master on Spiritual Leadership: ECK Leader's Guide, article 73

HU

HU, Law of. The first law of the physical universe. Spirit is the all-penetrating power which is the forming power of the universes of HU, the Voice of HU (God).

A Cosmic Sea of Words: The ECKANKAR Lexicon

HU, the secret name of God . . . can be chanted or sung quietly to yourself when you are in trouble or when you need consolation in time of grief. It gives strength, it gives health, it opens you as a channel for the greater healing of Divine Spirit.

How to Find God, **Mahanta Transcripts, Book 2, chap. 20**

The path of ECK is to lead an individual into a life that is spiritually uplifting and never degrading or depraved in any manner. It's supposed to build. When you get something on the inner—a direction to do something—if it's positive and harmonious, then do it. If you feel upset by it or if it demands that you exercise power over another person—in other words, the command you get means someone else loses his freedom to act as he wants to—then don't do it. It's the negative power, and it can even take the face of the ECK Master. Why? For our experience, so that we learn how to challenge it with one of the sacred words of God, such as HU. You can chant this quietly, and you can have protection. It opens you for this protection from Spirit.

This is one of the functions of HU, and it's a very

HU, the secret name of God . . . can be chanted or sung quietly to yourself when you are in trouble or when you need consolation in time of grief.

useful tool. You can do it at any time. If you need help—maybe somebody's gossiping or attacking you—you don't direct it at them but you just chant to uplift yourself spiritually so that you either gain an understanding or to protect yourself or whatever's needed.

How to Find God, **Mahanta Transcripts, Book 2, chap. 5**

Many of the different religious teachings have initiations. The Masonic order speaks of the lost word. This lost word actually is the sound of HU, or the Sound of God. This is one of the sacred names of God, which is a charged word. Such a word—and this includes our personal word—does not have power in itself. The word which we are given during the initiation acts like a key to unlock the protection and the spiritual help that is available from the ECK, or the Mahanta. We chant or sing this word, quietly or out loud, whenever we have need of this help.

How to Find God, **Mahanta Transcripts, Book 2, chap. 6**

The Sound of God, the Audible Life Stream, is the purifying element which uplifts Soul, so that one day It may return home to God, Its creator.

The Sound of God, the Audible Life Stream, is the purifying element which uplifts Soul, so that one day It may return home to God, Its creator.

How to Find God, **Mahanta Transcripts, Book 2, chap. 20**

HU, the secret name for God, has been brought out again. It is a pure word which hasn't been debased in profanity, like words such as *God.*

Cloak of Consciousness, **Mahanta Transcripts, Book 5, chap. 3**

The word *HU* has a purifying power for the individual.

Cloak of Consciousness, **Mahanta Transcripts, Book 5, chap. 3**

Sing HU every day.

The Spiritual Exercises of ECK are necessary to those who want the wisdom of ECK. Sing HU every day. You will begin to vibrate in tune with the Sound Current. Once you enter the rhythm of life, you *become* the Song of HU itself.

Wisdom from the Master on Spiritual Leadership:
ECK Leader's Guide, **article 9**

Life

life. Being; the experience of states of consciousness; life is Spirit, and Spirit is static; the Sound; the ECK.

A Cosmic Sea of Words: The ECKANKAR Lexicon

We begin to have experiences with the Light and Sound of God, and thus we develop a greater understanding of the spiritual laws of life. Knowing these laws, we can then make our own life easier.

The Dream Master, **Mahanta Transcripts, Book 8, chap. 8**

Each new experience, each new situation of life, widens the outlook of the chela and brings about a subtle transformation within himself. Thus the nature of every chela who is earnest and serious about the works of ECK is changing constantly, not only on account of the conditions of life, but by the constant addition of new impressions, the structure of the mind becomes ever more diverse and complex. Whether it is called progress or degeneration depends upon how one looks at it. But it has to be admitted that this is the law of life, in which the spiritual and the psychic coordinate and balance one another in the world of the spirito-materialistic, where Soul must serve out Its time for perfection.

The Shariyat-Ki-Sugmad, **Book Two, chap. 5**

Why me, Lord? is the age-old question we ask God. It is a form of prayer; it covers up our ignorance

We begin to have experiences with the Light and Sound of God, and thus we develop a greater understanding of the spiritual laws of life.

33

of the laws of life. Problems with life occur when we don't understand the laws of ECK—the laws of Spirit.

The Golden Heart, **Mahanta Transcripts, Book 4, chap. 1**

Problems with life occur when we don't understand the laws of ECK—the laws of Spirit.

Every issue of life is determined not by external conditions and things, but by one's consciousness. For example, the body in and of itself has no power, no intelligence, and is not responsible for its actions. A hand left to itself would remain where it is forever. There must be something to move it, and that something we call "I" or "Spirit." That "I" determines how the hand will be used; the hand cannot determine that in and of itself. The hand exists as an effect or as a form and responds to direction. As a vehicle or tool, it is obedient to us, and we impart to it whatever usefulness it has.

This idea can be applied to other parts of the body. The consciousness that formed the body in the beginning is the consciousness that maintains and sustains it. God gave us dominion through consciousness, and this consciousness, which is the creative principle of our body, must also be its sustaining and maintaining principle.

Once you have this principle, you have caught the entire principle of life. Literally, this is the Law of Life: the substance, the activity, the intelligent direction of life which is within man.

The Key to ECKANKAR, **pp. 18–19**

It is the law of all life to either progress or degenerate.

The Shariyat-Ki-Sugmad, **Book Two, chap. 10**

The Law of Life, or in a simpler term the Law of Realization, is that certain principle within each man

which reverses itself when man makes an effort to know God. You seek God in a manner, which
is not seeking It. You seek It by opening thy own inner self to It and letting It direct thy life as It desires.
It is an inner awareness that you gain through a certain relenting grace and understanding.

Stranger by the River, **chap. 31**

The law which all seek to know is the great
principle of life. Its simplicity is amazing for it is
summed up in the statement: Soul exists because
God loves It. In other words, all life exists because
God so wills it. This is the very foundation of life,
the whole of the philosophy of Eckankar. There is
nothing more and nothing less. All life is built upon
this basic principle of God. If Soul did not exist,
there would be no life anywhere on earth or on any
of the planets, nor on the various and many planes
throughout the universe of God.

The Shariyat-Ki-Sugmad, **Book One, chap. 8**

Respect for life must thus begin with us. Unless
we recognize and come to love ourselves as a special
being in the scheme of creation, we have a lot to
learn about the Law of Life that Rebazar revealed
to the seeker. You and I are Soul. In Its pure form,
nothing is more elegant or regal than Soul, for It
is the handiwork of the Creator. A saint, however,
is a model of humility.

The Master 4 Discourses, **lesson 10**

*At some point
in our lives,
our attitudes
and actions
come back to
us, giving each
of us the
experiences
that we have
earned.*

I'd always had the sense that the Law of Life
was just. And it is just. At some point in our lives,
our attitudes and actions come back to us, giving
each of us the experiences that we have earned. The

purpose of these experiences is to make us more conscious of why we are actually here. Gradually we learn that it's not just to tread water while we put in our time, it's to become a Co-worker with God.

The Drumbeat of Time, **Mahanta Transcripts, Book 10, chap. 5**

The Law of Life provides the way to higher consciousness as surely as the moth is given a way of out of the cocoon.

The Law of Life provides the way to higher consciousness as surely as the moth is given a way of out of the cocoon.

The Dream Master, **Mahanta Transcripts, Book 8, chap. 3**

I have no objections to someone doing whatever he has to do to survive, because whatever is done is balanced out with the Law of Life. There will come a time when life requires full payment for whatever was extracted from it.

The Book of ECK Parables, **Volume One, parable 2**

The Law of Life is that you must earn everything that you get in the true coin.

How the Inner Master Works, **Mahanta Transcripts, Book 12, chap. 10**

ECK does provide a shortcut to spiritual freedom, of course, but it is only a shortcut—not instant, undeserved entry. The Law of Life still requires that an individual repay as many of the karmic debts as needed to realize the reason for his troubles.

The Master 3 Discourses, **lesson 11**

The spiritual laws on each higher plane support the laws below, but are of a finer composition. In addition, there is a higher element to these laws, which often seems to be a reversal of the laws which the initiate has learned during his previous initiation. So he must come into agreement with the laws of the new plane which he has entered. In doing so, he learns to become more flexible, because life requires it of all who would reach the sanctuary of the Sugmad, the true Still Point.

The Master 2 Discourses, lesson 2

Look inwardly as you go to sleep tonight. Look for the guidance of the Holy Spirit, because this is the Voice of God. Look for the inner guide, the Dream Master, to show you how to understand the voice of the Holy Spirit as It comes to teach you how the laws of life can make yours a better one in every way.

We Come as Eagles, Mahanta Transcripts, Book 9, chap. 6

Look inwardly as you go to sleep tonight. Look for the guidance of the Holy Spirit, because this is the Voice of God.

This is the Law of Life, in that nothing is available unless you first obtain wisdom through the treasures stored within thyself. These in turn can be shared abundantly with others, bringing them happiness.

Stranger by the River, chap. 31

Mksha

Mksha, Law of. *MUHK-shah* Life is only Spirit, and being Spirit, it has nothing; it has only intelligence with the peculiar ability to perceive, penetrate, and survive, and have causation, specialization, creativeness, beauty, love, and ethics.

A Cosmic Sea of Words: The ECKANKAR Lexicon

There are fundamental laws that govern this physical universe through Spirit. These were once taught by an ancient ECK sage named Mksha, who appeared on this earth some 35,000 years ago to teach the people of the Indus Valley. His first teaching was, "Life is only Spirit, and being spirit it has nothing." The understanding of this points out clearly that it has only intelligence with the peculiar ability to perceive, penetrate, survive, have causation, specialization, creativeness, beauty, love, and ethics.

Spirit is the all-penetrating power which is the forming power of the universes of HU. It is the immortal unchanging source of life which only changes form regardless of what the world may be. It is the causative force which man has studied, written about, and can only know the exacting properties of, never actually acquiring total knowledge. We know that its modus operandi works peculiarly in exacting ways as do the mathematical formulas. Scientists and students of the holy works, all know this.

Spirit is the all-penetrating power which is the forming power of the universes. It is the immortal unchanging source of life.

The Flute of God, chap. 7

Physical Universe

laws of the physical universe. The Book of Laws; seven fundamental laws that govern the physical universe through Spirit: Law of Attitudes, Law of Facsimiles, Law of HU, Law of Polarity, Law of Soul, Law of Unity, and Law of Vibrations.

A Cosmic Sea of Words: The ECKANKAR Lexicon

These seven fundamental laws govern the physical universe through Divine Spirit, the ECK.

Law of HU: Spirit is the all-penetrating power which is the forming power of the universes of HU, the Voice of HU (God).

Law of Soul: Soul is the manifested individual beingness of the ECK Spirit (Holy Spirit); It has free will, opinions, intelligence, imagination, and immortality.

Law of Polarity: The Law of Opposites. The state of opposition between any two related forces; yin and yang (negative and positive), feminine and masculine; the negative, or reactive, side and the positive, or active, side; the third part is the passive, or middle, path; each thing in this universe is supported, animated, maintained by, and in opposition to its opposite.

Law of Vibrations: Governs all the influences upon Soul and the body in this world, such as wavelengths, outflows from the planets, stars, and heavenly bodies; music; sound; color; and general harmonics. Under this principle falls karma, cause and effect and inflow and outflow.

Law of Attitudes: Law of the States of Being; the

Soul is the manifested individual beingness of the ECK Spirit (Holy Spirit); It has free will, opinions, intelligence, imagination, and immortality.

41

power of imagination rules over will in the actions in this universe.

Law of Facsimiles: All effects in life are brought about by the thoughts and pictures in the mind of the individual.

Law of Unity: Thinking in the whole instead of the parts; a way of knowing the solution to a problem the instant it presents itself. This law simply means one must be wholly within the ECK (Holy Spirit) in order to enjoy himself as the whole man and be able to select consciously what he wants in life and work at it.

ECK Wisdom Temples, Spiritual Cities, & Guides:
A Brief History

Creativeness is only a deeper receptiveness.

One must come to realize that all creation is finished in the lower universes. Creativeness is only a deeper receptiveness. The entire contents of all time and all space, while experienced in a time sequence, actually coexist in an infinite and eternal *now.* In fact, all that mankind ever was or ever shall be in these lower worlds exists *now!* This is what is meant by the statement that creation is finished. Nothing is ever created, only manifested. What is called creativeness is only becoming aware of what already *is.* You simply become increasingly aware of portions of that which already exists.

The Key to ECKANKAR, p. 7

It is a law of the physical world that for a group to survive as long as possible, it must set up a seat of central government. For religions, this center is the hub for its spiritual activities, administration, and culture. Rightly or wrongly, people consider their seat of power the most important place on earth.

The Living Word, Book 2, chap. 28

Self

Self, Law of the. Each must understand and act to solve the mystery of their little self before they can solve the mystery of God.

A Cosmic Sea of Words: The ECKANKAR Lexicon

What is this law? I have written and spoken about it many times in the past, but it is important for a very good reason. It marks the place where Soul begins Its journey home to God. Note that.

The Living Word, **Book 2, chap. 35**

The seeker in *Stranger by the River* has done the right thing. In pursuit of truth, he has sought out the very best role model that Soul could hope to find: in this case, the ECK Master Rebazar Tarzs. . . . Who better, as a role model, than an ECK Master, who once also made his first halting steps to God Consciousness—but who finally reached it? . . .

And what does Rebazar tell the seeker?

"You, yourself, are your own problem," he says. "You must understand and act to solve the mystery of thy little self before you can solve the mystery of God."

The Living Word, **Book 2, chap. 35**

You must understand and act to solve the mystery of thy little self before you can solve the mystery of God.

So Rebazar says, "This is the law of the Self—the law of God. Therefore, I tell you not to take up the seeking of God until the little self within thee is conquered and solved."

Some signs that the little self is a stumbling stone to one's spiritual desire for God include, as Rebazar points out, a greater sense of outrage over the faults of others than at our own. Excusing our own weakness and shifting our blame to others. Liking gossip.

You may ask, "Well, what am I doing here on earth?"

That's like a child in school saying, "What am I doing here?"

Earth is a classroom. Its purpose is to help people develop (usually after many lifetimes) a godlike character.

Earth is a classroom. Its purpose is to help people develop (usually after many lifetimes) a god-like character.

The Living Word, **Book 2, chap. 35**

The problem most people have with life is that it beats them up terribly before their short span in it is finally at an end. They seldom have a sense of creating, of freedom, or even of love. Everything is duty. A chela (student) of ECK can have a bolder, more lively tomorrow by far, but he must be willing to create it for himself. No one else will do it for him. The Mahanta, the Living ECK Master will show the way and tell him where to locate the key to spiritual freedom. But each must retrieve his own key, for that is the Law of the Self.

Letters of Light & Sound 1, **lesson 5**

Soul

Soul, Law of. The second law of the physical universe. Soul is the manifested individual beingness of the ECK Spirit (Holy Spirit). It has free will, opinions, intelligence, imagination, and immortality.

A Cosmic Sea of Words: The ECKANKAR Lexicon

Soul is the manifested individual beingness of this ECK Spirit. The individual Soul has been created out of this Spirit, with the ability to have free will, to make its own choice, to be able to have opinions, intelligence, imagination, and to postulate and create.

The Flute of God, chap. 7

This means that all Souls who enter into the heavenly state must abide by the law which they establish for themselves. The self-abiding law is for the individual Soul to recognize that It is Its own law. First of all, It must love or give out goodwill to all beings within the heavenly worlds. Secondly, It must make Its own law to abide by, and this must be in harmony with the great law: Love all things.

The Shariyat-Ki-Sugmad, Book Two, chap. 7

All Souls who enter into the heavenly state must abide by the law which they establish for themselves, and this must be in harmony with the great law: Love all things.

We recognize that Soul is eternal; It has no beginning and no ending. Therefore, when a person

45

leaves this physical body, he continues to exist, usually on a higher plane of consciousness.

How to Find God, **Mahanta Transcripts,
Book 2, chap. 4**

Soul, at Its best, responds only to the higher laws of ECK. It will obey them without fail, even as the wolf unfailingly obeys the laws of its own nature.

The Eternal Dreamer, **Mahanta Transcripts,
Book 7, chap. 1**

Always remember that you are Soul. In that state of consciousness you can get unlimited help from the Mahanta.

Wisdom from the Master on Spiritual Leadership:
ECK Leader's Guide, **article 54**

The higher Soul goes and the more freedom It gets, the more responsibility It has.

The spiritual principle is that Soul is free. And with that freedom comes responsibility. The higher Soul goes and the more freedom It gets, the more responsibility It has. And the higher you go, you also see how little freedom other people have—and they don't even know it.

Wisdom from the Master on Spiritual Leadership:
ECK Leader's Guide, **article 63**

Spirit

Spirit, Law of. Spirit, in Itself, is the principle of increase; future conditions grow out of present conditions; there is always something more to come, another experience to experience.

A Cosmic Sea of Words: The ECKANKAR Lexicon

Self-mastery simply means that a person has the ability to run his own life according to the laws of Spirit. This presumes, first of all, that you know the laws of Spirit. The understanding of these laws comes through the Light and Sound of God; it is a direct infusion of the Shariyat-Ki-Sugmad into Soul.

The Golden Heart, **Mahanta Transcripts, Book 4, chap. 5**

Spirit is the all-penetrating power which is the forming power of the universes of HU. It is the immortal unchanging source of life which only changes form regardless of what the world may be. . . .

This Spirit, the Voice of HU—HU is often known as the Sugmad—which is the true name of God in the upper realms, has one great quality and that is to create effect. As It flows down through the worlds, from Its fountainhead in the center of all creation, far above this earth world, It needs distributors, and It works through Souls.

The Flute of God, **chap. 7**

Self-mastery simply means that a person has the ability to run his own life according to the laws of Spirit.

This only means that God of Itself is Being, and Spirit is that extension of It into all universes, and you, as the instrument, are Spirit made flesh.

The Key to ECKANKAR, p. 8

Our name for Spirit is simply ECK. This ECK is what the Bible refers to as the Holy Ghost, the Comforter. This is the same manifestation that came to the apostles at Pentecost. They heard a sound like a rushing wind. This is one of the sounds of Spirit. There are many more, such as the sound of the flute.

How to Find God, Mahanta Transcripts, Book 2, chap. 4

The Sound and Light are the twin aspects of Spirit. This is the Voice of God.

The Sound and Light are the twin aspects of Spirit. This is the Voice of God. There are three parts, actually, that we are interested in as we step on the spiritual path. First there is thought. We use our mind and the imaginative techniques in working with the Spiritual Exercises of ECK. With the Spiritual Exercises of ECK, we consciously try to make contact with this Light and Sound of God. It's a worthwhile goal to experience the Voice of God: It means we have contact with the Divinity.

How to Find God, Mahanta Transcripts, Book 2, chap. 5

In ECK, the individual is instructed in the laws of Spirit. How he uses this knowledge determines how soon he enters the joyful state of God Enlightenment, which can be attained while still in the human body.

The Living Word, Book 1, chap. 5

Use prudence with your defects—and I love you with or without them. However, I also love those whom you injure by your thoughtless deeds. The Law of ECK binds me to protect them.

Wisdom of the Heart, **Book 1, Wisdom Note 4**

Personal rules lead to a choice of which area to give service to God and life, but our rules must agree with the laws of Divine Spirit.

The Master 4 Discourses, **lesson 11**

Spiritual Evolution

Spiritual Evolution, Law of. Presupposes inequality in all things and beings and their continued effort for self-improvement in life.

A Cosmic Sea of Words: The ECKANKAR Lexicon

This creative process depends upon the spiritual unfoldment of Soul and the degree of Its
awakened consciousness. . . . This is also in accord
with the Law of Spiritual Evolution, which presupposes inequality in all things and beings and their
continued effort for self-improvement in life.

The Spiritual Notebook, **chap. 4**

This creative process depends upon the spiritual unfoldment of Soul.

Spiritual Nonperfection

Spiritual Nonperfection, Law of.   No one ever becomes a perfect being; there is always one more step in God's plan of conscious evolution.

A Cosmic Sea of Words: The ECKANKAR Lexicon

"The Law of Spiritual Nonperfection holds that no one ever becomes a perfect being." There is always one more step in God's plan of conscious evolution. This is all the more true of spiritual things which always seek, but never find, completion.

Child in the Wilderness, **chap. 27**

There is always one more step in God's plan of conscious evolution.

Strength

Strength, Law of.   Only the strong enter the kingdom of heaven.

A Cosmic Sea of Words: The ECKANKAR Lexicon

The Law of Strength says that only the strong
enter the kingdom of heaven. This spiritual strength
is developed through the disciplines, customs, and
practices set up by the Mahanta to separate illusion
from truth for the seeker. Among the chief of all
precepts in ECK is the need to do the Spiritual
Exercises of ECK; these are mainly to give Soul the
recognition of Itself as a channel for the Mahanta
and allow It to become secure in the Sound and
Light of Sugmad. This comprises the Law of
Strength.

Soul Travel 1—The Illuminated Way, **lesson 3**

*This spiritual
strength is
developed
through the
disciplines,
customs, and
practices set
up by the
Mahanta to
separate
illusion from
truth for the
seeker.*

The connection between the inner and outer
teachings is that Soul is strengthened and
emboldened by the rigors of trials on the physical
level that try to shake It loose from the Tree of Life.

The Living Word, **Book 1, chap. 12**

Suffering could build strength, but only if a
person acknowledges his or her responsibility for
whatever went wrong.

Sometimes you can't. Sometimes what goes
wrong in this life is caused by something you did
in your last lifetime. If you don't remember, you're

not able to connect cause and effect. . . .

How do you know when you're getting stronger? Other people can often tell better than you, yourself. A humble person wouldn't even put attention on that because it's inside yourself. The only way you really know if you're stronger is if you go through a time of hardship and you get through it somehow by listening. You trust something inside yourself— the strength you have gained to this point.

The Drumbeat of Time, Mahanta Transcripts, Book 10, chap. 12

Spiritual strength cannot be separated from the moral qualities of mankind.

The Living Word, Book 1, chap. 12

Each hardship and trial is actually there as a gift from God, to make you stronger.

Every knockdown in life is teaching you to be stronger, to stand more sturdily. Each hardship and trial is actually there as a gift from God, to make you stronger. If people understood this, they wouldn't complain so much.

What Is Spiritual Freedom? Mahanta Transcripts, Book 11, chap. 10

Only the strong can stand the true love of God.

What Is Spiritual Freedom? Mahanta Transcripts, Book 11, chap. 11

Survival

Survival, Law of. Each must take care of himself by earning his own way in society; Soul must keep growing.

A Cosmic Sea of Words: The ECKANKAR Lexicon

My spiritual duty is to help you, the ECK initiate, understand the spiritual laws of ECK that apply to everyone. If the law of your country provides for you in times of need, accept the aid as long as necessary. But when you can take care of yourself, by earning your own way in society, you owe it to yourself to do so. The Law of Survival, like any of the laws of ECK, often appears to forget the offender. But the grace period does end.

Wisdom of the Heart, **Book 2, Wisdom Note 8**

Soul must keep growing. When you can take care of yourself, by earning your own way in society, you owe it to yourself to do so.

If you give to others of your goods or time with an attitude of love and goodwill, you act in God's name. If you find yourself in need of help, accept the aid of others with grace. But if you later can repay them, it is a spiritual duty to do so. Life requires that each repay his debts to others—here and now, in this lifetime.

Do it soon. Later could mean another lifetime.

Wisdom of the Heart, **Book 2, Wisdom Note 8**

As we get older, our bodies don't respond the same way they used to. That means the foods and the nutrition that we were used to just aren't

Sometimes when people retire, they forget to keep growing in the areas of survival.

adequate anymore. Survival is a day-by-day lesson. It means you've got to keep learning, retired or not. Sometimes when people retire, they forget to keep growing in the areas of survival. They forget to ask, "How do I eat better?" or "What better nutrition do I need now? What isn't in the soil today that used to be there in 1940 when good food came straight from the land?" Things have changed. You've got to keep growing, because that's part of the spiritual law of survival.

Our Spiritual Wake-Up Calls, **Mahanta Transcripts, Book 15, chap. 10**

Three Basic Principles of Eckankar

Three Basic Principles of Eckankar. First, Soul is eternal; It has no beginning or end. Second, whosoever travels the high path of ECK dwells in the spiritual planes. Third, Soul always lives in the present; It has no past and no future.

A Cosmic Sea of Words: The ECKANKAR Lexicon

By now he begins to see the wisdom of the three basic principles of ECK. First, Soul is eternal. It has no beginning nor ending. Second, whosoever travels the high path of ECK always dwells in the spiritual planes. Third, Soul always lives in the present. It has no past and no future, but always lives in the present moment.

The Shariyat-Ki-Sugmad, **Book Two, chap. 12**

Every Soul is the spiritual spark of God invested in a physical body. The body does not have to die for Soul to reach the spiritual universe during the time that It resides upon earth. Man does not have to become anything other than what he is in order to have divine guidance, divine protection, divine wisdom, and divine understanding through the Living ECK Master. He must recognize only that God is and that he himself, as Soul, also is.

Soul is never anything else but this. It is always in eternity. It is always in the present NOW. It is

Every Soul is the spiritual spark of God invested in a physical body.

59

always in the heavenly state of God. These are the three principles of Eckankar which It must come to understand and know well. Out of these principles springs the doctrine and philosophy of ECK. There is nothing more to say and there is nothing less to say.

By the realization of these three principles the chela becomes a transparency for the divine impulse.

By the realization of these three principles the chela becomes a transparency for the divine impulse. He comes into a greater awareness of the divine plan in this world, and his part in it. He now rests in the arms of the Mahanta, the Inner ECK Master, and relies upon him to give him his divine guidance.

As he rises higher in this spiritual realization, the great discovery of life is found. The majestic law of God upon which the three principles of ECK rest is that "Soul exists because the Sugmad wills it."

The Shariyat-Ki-Sugmad, Book One, chap. 8

We see the height of the mountains and the depths of the valleys, because the only way anything can be known in these lower worlds is in comparison to its opposite.

Laws of Freedom

The practical laws that afford a smoother passage through everyday life

Assumption

Assumption, Law of. It is only by living each moment in the assumption of one's divinity that an individual can bring his spiritual potential into the world.

A Cosmic Sea of Words: The ECKANKAR Lexicon

Soul, in waking from Its languor, begins a search for truth. The individual first seeks the Mahanta on the inner planes, because the spiritual law requires a recognition of the agent of God. After that, the spiritual forces converge. This law further states that whatever takes place inside us may later become a reality in this physical world.

Letters of Light & Sound 2, **lesson 12**

The question always arises: What should I do if I am consciously dreaming or on a different plane and I want to get back into the awareness of the physical body? There is one basic rule: Assume with the sense of feeling that you are in your physical body. This will happen immediately.

The Spiritual Exercises of ECK, **spir. ex. 12**

When you have a bad dream, the dream censor has not allowed the whole story to come out. Begin with the assumption that something's missing, that you don't know everything yet. Then use the inner faculties to get the answers you need.

The Book of ECK Parables, **Volume 3, parable 32**

It is only by living each moment in the assumption of one's divinity that an individual can bring his spiritual potential into the world.

Attitudes

Attitudes, Law of.   The fifth law of the physical universe, or Law of the States of Being; the power of imagination rules over will in the actions in this universe.

A Cosmic Sea of Words: The ECKANKAR Lexicon

We know that there is an answer for every situation that comes up in our life. There is always a way, somehow. What holds us back is our attitudes. Learn the value of doing a spiritual exercise just before retiring or upon awakening. It works to your advantage during these times of change in conscious awareness.

The Art of Spiritual Dreaming, **chap. 11**

The fifth law of the physical universe is the Law of Attitudes, or the states of being. Frankly, everything that operates with the laws of this part is capable of performing miracles. Not will, but the power of imagination rules our actions in this universe.

The Flute of God, **chap. 7**

Lai Tsi says, "I have learned to stand back and let the divine work through me." We find that this is the simple way of doing it. . . .

I found when adopting a certain attitude that I made contact with this power. It was an attitude of curious, childlike devotion to the great Spirit. . . .

We know that there is an answer for every situation that comes up in our life. There is always a way, somehow. What holds us back is our attitudes.

67

So many people want this childlike state but the urgency of their physical needs causes tension and fear thus closing the channel between themselves and the Spirit. Anxiety and fear are tense emotions, fastening the person rigidly into the emotional plane of consciousness so that he cannot reach the spiritual plane where things come true.

Competition intensifies the attitude of tension; tension springs from fear; fear rises out of excessive self-love; excessive self-love cuts one off from the contact with the ECK; thus, the qualities leading to satisfaction, happiness and growth are not achieved. . . .

Anyone who recognizes his own self, as Soul, relaxes at once, for he can truly say, "I and the Father are one."

In this relaxed way, all channels from within are opened.

The Flute of God, chap. 7

This is the same way life works. When we think, when we image something in our minds, we are sighting pictures in the viewfinder of the mind.

Briefly, the Law of Attitudes goes like this. It is the corrected feeling and pictures you carry in your mind constantly. If you decide to take a picture with a camera—let's say of a tree, and do so, you view the pictured tree in the viewfinder. After a few days you get the pictures back from the camera shop, and you are not surprised to find that it's really a picture of a tree you took.

This is, simply, the same way life works. When we think, when we image something in our minds, we are sighting pictures in the viewfinder of the mind. The thought vibrations within us will deal with the exposed films we have made and presently the finished picture comes into visibility in our lives. It's as simple as that.

The Flute of God, chap. 7

Every present thought solidifies into a future condition.

Dialogues with the Master, chap. 8

Every present thought solidifies into a future condition.

Remember that the subtle forces within man are the same, but the important thing is the manner in which we call upon it. If we speak to it in negative terms, it responds in that manner. We impose self-limitations upon ourselves to give the power an opportunity to work through the subconscious mind.

Dialogues with the Master, chap. 10

Whatever is in the consciousness is bound to come forth. . . .

It can be compulsive or of the free will. The covert negative attitudes that one has against another or against certain segments of life will leap out in time. For example, if a person has many covert attitudes against men and women, it is doubtful if he can confront his fellowmen. This is the type of person who spends too much time alone.

Don't do too many things with people of this nature, like precipitating their anger, because it will definitely pull their triggers and they will go down the dwindling spiral in a hurry. Some cases are suicides. The karma created out of some action against someone else keeps the individuals in a constant quarrel, mainly with themselves. Many times they believe they are quarreling with another, but it is with themselves.

The Key to ECKANKAR, p. 19

In ECK we understand that the mind runs in a rut. We pick up habits as children, which carry into the teen years and become hardened and so-lidified as we grow older. Anger and other attitudes of the mind stem from these habits. The only thing that is greater than mind is Soul. It is above the power of the mind, and It is the only thing able to nudge the mind out of its rut.

The only thing that is greater than mind is Soul. It is above the power of the mind, and It is the only thing able to nudge the mind out of its rut.

How to Find God, **Mahanta Transcripts, Book 2, chap. 2**

This is the attitude we take in life on the path to God. We don't say, "I'm afraid to step out in life because I'll be shown up as ignorant." We step out boldly and courageously. We learn things. We're willing to make a fool of ourself just for the sake of experience or learning.

How to Find God, **Mahanta Transcripts, Book 2, chap. 2**

The mind with its routines and habits doesn't want to change what it has been doing. It wants to keep reading and enjoying itself. But Spirit moves on, and the mind and emotions and everything else move along. If we aren't willing to exercise this randomity . . . , we have a hard time through our initiations.

Going from one initiation level to the next ought to be a very easy and smooth transition. We have to be willing to let go of old attitudes and stay very open to Spirit as It tries to lead us into greater awareness. Once you have opened up to Spirit, the Inner Master will step in—as long as you give per-mission—and take you into the greater vistas. If Soul has given permission but the lower bodies don't know it, this is when you start saying you've got all these problems.

Now is the time to start giving of yourself. It

doesn't necessarily have to be within the ECK program, but you have to begin giving back to life in some way. Do this according to your own talents and interests. Some people like to give talks, others don't; they're petrified. If that's the case, then don't give talks. Some like to work with children, while others—maybe those who have been parents—may say, I've done my time; let someone else have a turn.

How to Find God, **Mahanta Transcripts, Book 2, chap. 5**

A mind with randomity . . . can change under any circumstance—this is a factor which isn't very well known. But the higher Soul travels on the spiritual path, the less become Its burdens, and the easier it is to change swiftly from one course to another. A mind that moves with random speed works in the field of randomity.

The Key to ECKANKAR, **p. 9**

We do not have to please God, we have to manifest Its presence.

Many who are doing good have little or no idea as to what good really is. Many are willing to have God interfere in their lives, but are not willing to do what is needed for themselves. However, when anyone examines his life, he will come to the realization that it is always his beliefs, considerations, and conditionings that determine his experiences in life.

So we come to the most important part of life's message: It is not what we do that determines our experience in life, but it is what we expect! Even when you have done all the correct things, if you have the haunting fear that things will go wrong,

It is not what we do that determines our experience in life, but it is what we expect!

they will go wrong. Is it because you are bad, sinful, or evil? No. It is because you have that belief.

The Key to ECKANKAR, p. 14

It is I AM's concept of Itself that determines the form and scenery of Its existence. Everything depends upon Its attitude towards Itself; that which It will not affirm as true of Itself cannot awaken in Its world.

The Key to ECKANKAR, p. 6

To develop this creative imagination, work with the Spiritual Exercises of ECK.

We know that we can shape our future. . . . because the future is unformed. You can make it what you want, but first you have to be able to visualize what you want very clearly. Unfortunately, most people look for materialistic goals such as money, health, wealth, and companionship. But again I'm going to mention this: As Jesus said, "Seek ye first the Kingdom of God . . . and all these things shall be added unto you." Make sure that your goal is worth the trouble.

To develop this creative imagination, work with the Spiritual Exercises of ECK. Experiment freely with these techniques. What you're looking for is to have experience with the Sound and Light, where you will have adventures in the other worlds.

How to Find God, **Mahanta Transcripts, Book 2, chap. 4**

Balance

Balance, Law of. The stability which lies in the Godhead: all is completely in balance in God's universal body. The principle of unity, or oneness, but in the lower worlds this unity is simulated by the interchange between the pairs of opposites.

A Cosmic Sea of Words: The ECKANKAR Lexicon

Blindness to cause and effect is still man's relentless problem today. The human consciousness refuses to admit that all actions have consequences. The Living ECK Master demonstrates the Law of Balance in terms of contemporary customs.

The Living Word, **Book 1, chap. 25**

Blindness to cause and effect is still man's relentless problem today.

As we live the life of ECK, we want to know how It works in our daily life. A professional musician recently said he had developed a case of jittery nerves. So much of this creative flow was coming through him that he was not able to take the time to balance it with some kind of physical activity. . . . He's so involved with his music that he has not been able to work any physical activity into his daily schedule.

Another musician told about joining a basketball team. The musician was able to get his exercise in this way. It is important to keep a balance in our physical life. When we get the ECK flowing in, all too often we want to put all of our attention on the

73

books of ECK or the contemplative exercises, and we forget that we also have to live day to day.

How to Find God, **Mahanta Transcripts, Book 2, chap. 3**

We have times when everything is going our way, but there are also times when we're at the bottom. If we keep ourselves open to Spirit, there will be an equal balance.

Life goes up and down. We have times when everything is going our way, but there are also times when we're at the bottom. If we keep ourselves open to Spirit, there will be an equal balance. This is what is meant by the detached state: When our fortunes hit bottom, we surrender to Spirit. Then we can go back up more naturally, and we'll maintain this rhythm of life. As life goes on around us, the detached state is that which runs right through the center; we are the balanced individual working in the Soul consciousness.

How to Find God, **Mahanta Transcripts, Book 2, chap. 3**

We do what we can, but we don't feel guilty and we don't let ourselves get out of balance. We work with other like-minded people to accomplish things; we don't sit back in life and just wash our hands of the whole affair.

How to Find God, **Mahanta Transcripts, Book 2, chap. 4**

You get to the Soul Plane by balancing the positive and the negative parts within yourself; they come into perfect balance on the Soul Plane. From this moment on we have Self-Realization. . . . This is a spiritual transfiguration that occurs—you actually become a new person. You are now in the state of self-recognition: knowing who you are, what you are, and what your mission in life may be.

How to Find God, **Mahanta Transcripts, Book 2, chap. 4**

Each Soul is an individual and unique being. In the lower planes we have the two parts of our lower nature: the positive and the negative. When we get to the Soul Plane, we find that these two parts become one. This is called the self-recognition state, what Socrates referred to when he said, "Man, know thyself." Up until this time, knowing the self meant merely knowing the ego, or the little self, rather than our true spiritual nature. Our consciousness changes when we reach the Soul Plane; we now have an outlook on life that is balanced.

In the dream state, marriage simply means that Soul is having an inner initiation where the two parts of Itself are drawn a little closer together. We are looking for the linkup of Soul with the ECK, this Divine Spirit which comes from God. Each time you see a marriage on the inner planes, regardless of the personality you perceive as your mate, it means a closer marriage with Spirit and with God.

How to Find God, **Mahanta Transcripts, Book 2, chap. 12**

We don't want to practice austerities; that is not balance. Buddha spoke about this. He had started out his life as a rich young man, protected from seeing poverty or sorrow; and when he went out into the world, he said, Now I must beg and become poor. He tried fasting, and that didn't work out so well. All he got was skinny as a rail. After a while he said there must be some way to live a life that is well balanced. There must be a middle way.

In the spiritual life, we look to find the balance so that when we have this experience of God and see the Light—whether It is the Blue Light or anything else—we are able to carry on. We don't get frantic and say, Will I ever see It again? When the

We don't want to practice austerities; that is not balance.

time is right, you will. Others will hear the Sound. These are the two aspects of God which the ECKists, and even those who aren't in Eckankar outwardly, are beginning to learn about and experience in their daily life.

How to Find God, Mahanta Transcripts, Book 2, chap. 14

There is a natural cycle that we run: activity, rest, activity, rest. An ECKist learns how to walk the middle path where he can make the activity and rest work for him, so that he becomes a conscious Co-worker with God twenty-four hours a day.

Someone mentioned they didn't know how to find people with motivation or how to motivate them. And really you can't. You find people who are motivated at any particular moment. Some are motivated for awhile, and then they go into a rest period—the rest points in eternity. There is a natural cycle that we run: activity, rest, activity, rest. An ECKist learns how to walk the middle path where he can make the activity and rest work for him, so that he becomes a conscious Co-worker with God twenty-four hours a day.

How to Find God, Mahanta Transcripts, Book 2, chap. 21

All events and experiences in life reflect the Law of Spiritual Balance. Sooner or later, the pendulum swings back. That moment, when major positive and negative forces are in equal proportions, we may refer to as "On the edge of eternity."

It means having a chance to go beyond the normal cause and effect of daily experience.

The Master 4 Discourses, lesson 7

Connecting Diamonds

connecting diamonds. Events are like diamonds. Invisible lines connect them, a part of a divine plan. The God lover learns to see and follow these lines, for they smooth his way. They lead over holy ground. It is there that the Holy Spirit does the wonders that help an individual do what he cannot do alone. It shields him. Its love and mercy are the grace that put joy and goodness into everyday life.

A Cosmic Sea of Words: The ECKANKAR Lexicon

Events are like diamonds. Invisible lines connect them, a part of a divine plan.

There is a spiritual principle called connecting diamonds that is at work every day of our lives, whether we are aware of it or not. . . .

Let's look at an example:

An old friend of an ECKist came to town for a visit. The two decided to find a billiard parlor and enjoy an afternoon of billiards. They looked in the phone directory, found the location of a few places, then set out for one. Although they had agreed to try the first place on their list, the driver was actually en route to the second location before either noticed the error. So they turned around. To save time, and with map in hand, they took a shortcut along some unfamiliar streets. Soon they reached their destination. But the billiard tables were all full, which meant either waiting for a table or else trying to find another parlor with an open table. So they left.

They climbed back into the car, checked the map, then set out for the second choice on their list—a location many miles distant, on the other side of town.

By an odd coincidence, the second place happened to be on the very same street. However, this fact was not apparent to them as they drove, because their route ran along city streets, onto a freeway, then back onto city streets again. But this second billiard parlor, which the driver had instinctively set out for at the start, was on the same street as the first, although many miles apart.

That is an example of connecting diamonds.

It works like this: We perceive of some idea that we feel will enrich our life at that very moment. We make a plan. Then we set out from home to accomplish the first leg of our search, but find the ECK is actually trying to get us to go directly to the second place. We resist the guidance of the Holy Spirit. We check our original plans (road map) again and try to find a shortcut to the place we think we should be at. When we arrive, nothing works out.

The trip is not a loss, however, unless we become discouraged and head straight home.

Most people don't know that life connects.

But giving up is too easy. If, instead, we decide to pursue our original plan, we will bring out the map again and try to find a new route to our destination. In doing so, we often find that a line connects all the main points in our quest. Individuals who know and follow this principle of connecting diamonds are usually happy and successful in life.

The Living Word, **Book 2, chap. 5**

Every event in our life is part of a divine plan that accounts for each so-called mistake or happening of chance. Most people don't know that life connects. They don't realize that the events in their lives are diamonds and that invisible lines run between them in every possible direction and combination of points. To be happy, we must take the initiative to connect those points that bring love and goodness to us.

How do you start?

You cannot ever put too much emphasis upon having a spiritual frame of mind. So begin every day with the Spiritual Exercises of ECK. Sing HU or your personal word. The spiritual exercises will give you the strongest connection of all—a bond with the ECK, the Holy Spirit.

Second, sit back and dream the sort of life you would like. What would you like to do? To be? Think backward from the goal of your desire. That will be your plan for achievement.

Third, begin.

That's looking at your plan for spiritual happiness and success from end to beginning. Now let's look at it more logically. There will be three stages, or connecting diamonds, to this plan. First, you must do something, or make a beginning. But where? In what direction? Until you know the third, or final, point of the connecting diamonds (your goal), you cannot begin to work toward that end. So see a picture of your goal.

You'll notice that an uncomfortable space still lies between step one, the starting point, and the third step, your goal. This middle point is the unformed, creative part where the Holy Spirit works Its wonders to help you accomplish what you cannot do yourself.

How do you get moving?

You'll never get to this miraculous part of life until you set a goal. Then you must take the initiative and begin to move toward it. Only then will the

The spiritual exercises will give you the strongest connection of all—a bond with the ECK, the Holy Spirit.

Holy Spirit help you through the large, unknown second area, where you must exercise your talents to create a better life for yourself.

Paul Twitchell speaks about the diamond. In *The ECK-Vidya, Ancient Science of Prophecy,* he says: "The diamond . . . is related to the physical world and man's human experience. It represents divine power brought to bear upon the material conditions. Intuition, clairvoyance, inspiration are faculties of the higher mind whereby light is reflected as from a flawless diamond."

Do you want to be happy? Then set out to learn about the connecting diamonds in your own life. They shimmer and glisten all around you.

But always begin your search by singing HU, or some other love song to God.

Always begin your search by singing HU, or some other love song to God.

The Living Word, **Book 2, chap. 5**

Destiny

Destiny, Law of. Soul comes into the world to accomplish an assortment of tasks; these assignments taken as a whole make up Its destiny.

A Cosmic Sea of Words: The ECKANKAR Lexicon

Soul enters this world to accomplish a collection of tasks. Taken as a whole, these assignments make up Its destiny. To set the tone for Its mission, Soul may come into either a healthy body or a sickly one; into comfortable means or poverty; with great intellect or a simple mind; with the favored color of skin for that era or not; once a male, again a female.

Destiny, as a concept, is waning in popularity in Western society today. People want to run their own lives. They want to shape their own tomorrows.

Autobiography of a Modern Prophet, **chap. 3**

Soul enters this world to accomplish a collection of tasks. Taken as a whole, these assignments make up Its destiny.

The primal seed for each incarnation is under the umbrella of destiny, known to us also as past-life karma. On a practical level, genetic, cultural, and social elements combine to determine Soul's position in this world. For people on the lower end of the survival scale, the Lord of Karma alone chooses the time and place of rebirth. By definition, the survival scale is a yardstick of one's can-do instincts. But karmic placement does allow some people a voice in their place of birth. These are the individuals near the top of the scale, who are always creative in some way—usually cheerful, upbeat people. Because of gains made in past-life unfoldment, they have won a say in choosing their present incarnation.

Destiny can be thought of as the equipment, talents, or gifts which a person brings to this life. It remains for each to use them wisely.

Autobiography of a Modern Prophet, **chap. 3**

Destiny can be thought of as the equipment, talents, or gifts which a person brings to this life. It remains for each to use them wisely.

Once an individual makes a commitment to hold true to the teachings of ECK and follow the words of the Living ECK Master, it is a sure thing he will see his outer life run in new directions. The Law of Destiny, which has dictated the direction of his life to this point, is dismantled. The power is taken from that mechanism. A whole new chapter is begun when the Master turns the page in the Book of Life. Whatever is expected when one begins an earnest study in ECK, it is certain that the love of the Sound Current is smoldering in the center of the spirit.

The ECK Satsang Discourses, **Third Series, lesson 6**

Detachment

detachment. Giving up strong affection for the environment and possessions, but not ceasing to identify with them; becoming independent of them; mentally free from love of the world and all worldly desires.

A Cosmic Sea of Words: The ECKANKAR Lexicon

Detachment is something we know about in the spiritual life. It doesn't mean not to get involved; it means to not let outer circumstances throw off your inner balance.

The Art of Spiritual Dreaming, **chap. 9**

The word *detachment* is too cold. What is meant in spiritual terms is this—we, as one with all, will have a certain amount of pleasure and pain, but will not let it affect our emotional balance too greatly to throw our minds into the extreme poles of joy or sorrow. The real control is detachment from fear. Once you have gained this important attribute of God, then you can enjoy greater life. Yes, you can have a joy mixed with pain and not be affected to the same extent as previously. Only when fear is in control of those two poles is your life attached to its physical, mental, and spiritual possessions. Give up fear and you need never give up another thing in your life. Great joys physically, mentally, and spiritually can become yours, balanced by what sorrows there need be in your life!

Give up fear and you need never give up another thing in your life.

Dialogues with the Master, **chap. 13**

The razor's edge is one's calm detachment from the things of this world; yet he may enjoy them as a blessing of life, for past karma has brought them for his experience. There is no virtue in suffering, poverty, or martyrdom, unless the individual needs those experiences for the purification of Soul.

The Living Word, Book 1, chap. 32

One must be detached from all love of material things and events, from all concern about them. The chela attains this attitude—because his love is centered above the perishable things of this world—and reaches the heavenly planes.

From the love of objects of the senses man has desires; from his desires rises anger. From anger proceeds delusion, and from delusion come confused memories and senses. This destroys his love of God, and from all this he perishes. But when he is disciplined and places his love in the Mahanta, then does he move among the objects of his senses free from pleasures and free from pain, but mostly free from self-indulgence.

The Shariyat-Ki-Sugmad, Book One, chap. 7

Charity is what the Christian Bible speaks of as good will. We call it vairag, or detachment.

How to Find God, Mahanta Transcripts, Book 2, chap. 4

The vairag is the detached state of consciousness. This goes along with God-Realization. Detached does not mean without compassion, uncaring, without love. It means simply that you can have compassion, you can enjoy life, but if sorrow comes into your life,

Detached does not mean without compassion, uncaring, without love. It means simply that you can have compassion, you can enjoy life, but if sorrow comes into your life, it does not burden you until the end of your days.

it does not burden you until the end of your days. You are able to see the hand of God in it.

How to Find God, **Mahanta Transcripts,**
Book 2, chap. 2

There are a few individuals who do drink from this water of immortality; they learn to work with the enzymes and to reverse the aging process because they have a mission. They are not concerned about staying in the body or not. They just do their work. The person who qualifies is one who learns to work in the state of vairag, or detachment. This does not mean giving up all interest in the family, throwing away all emotions and walking through life like a zombie, a computer-controlled robot, and then saying, I am now in the detached state. No. One who does that is actually in the sleep state.

Journey of Soul, **Mahanta Transcripts,**
Book 1, chap. 14

Detached means seeing the play of life—crying when we must, laughing when we can—but at all times looking at life from the viewpoint of Soul, knowing that even this shall pass away.

How to Find God, **Mahanta Transcripts,**
Book 2, chap. 17

We have the attitude of total trust in life to give us what is for our own spiritual benefit.

Detached does not mean unemotional; it means that no matter what we have in life, we will not be crushed if it is taken from us. It means we have the attitude of total trust in life to give us what is for our own spiritual benefit.

How to Find God, **Mahanta Transcripts,**
Book 2, chap. 22

Discrimination

discrimination. The recognition that there is no good nor evil, no beauty nor ugliness, no sin, and that these are concepts of the mind, the dual forces in the matter worlds; the ability to make right judgments; to distinguish between those actions which contribute to spiritual growth and those which are a waste of time.

A Cosmic Sea of Words: The ECKANKAR Lexicon

viveka. The first step in Eckankar; right discrimination; being able to discriminate between what will be good for spiritual advancement or would be wasting time; the opposite of kama, lust.

A Cosmic Sea of Words: The ECKANKAR Lexicon

It requires a high level of discrimination to avoid breaking the spiritual law.

The ECK Satsang Discourses, **Fourth Series, lesson 12**

In order to know when to speak and when to remain silent, you must apply the Law of Discrimination.

A Modern Prophet Answers Your Key Questions about Life, **chap. 3**

Discrimination just means making the right choices.

Discrimination just means making the right choices. Some people have an uncanny knack for making the wrong choices, and that's why they have the problems they do. They'll get into one unhappy marriage after another after another. Two, three, four times the mate turns out to be an alcoholic. You say, "What bad luck!" But it's not bad luck. Soul, who is making the choice, has poor discrimination and makes poor choices.

How do you change this? First you have to look at your own weaknesses. Then you have to also know how to grow and develop spiritually. Generally it's through singing the ancient name of God, HU. This or one of the other spiritual exercises helps.

Our Spiritual Wake-Up Calls, **Mahanta Transcripts, Book 15, chap. 4**

As you grow in discrimination, you learn you can only accept a certain amount of something. Then you have to step back and say, "I'll learn to do things another way." You fall back on your creativity—the creativity of Soul.

The Secret of Love, **Mahanta Transcripts, Book 14, chap. 9**

Unless we have opened our heart through singing HU, we won't have the discrimination to know wisdom when we hear it.

The Razor's Edge of discrimination always hounds a seeker of God.

The Living Word, **Book 1, chap. 32**

God speaks through dreams, intuition, and sometimes the voices of other people who have more experience than we do. But unless we have opened our heart through singing HU, we won't have the discrimination to know wisdom when we hear it.

The Drumbeat of Time, **Mahanta Transcripts, Book 10, chap. 13**

Economy

Economy, Law of. Using our resources to the fullest; no matter what thought we have or what action we take, it results in the most productive deed we can do as Soul learning to become a Co-worker with God.

A Cosmic Sea of Words: The ECKANKAR Lexicon

There is something that I have been watching and studying for years, and it's one of the laws that is rarely mentioned. It's called the Law of Economy. The principle is referred to in some of the ECK books, but without that title. It merely means that you get the most mileage out of every gallon of gas.

The Secret Teachings, **Mahanta Transcripts, Book 3, chap. 4**

The Law of Economy merely means that you get the most mileage out of every gallon of gas.

The Law of Economy is the ECK in expression. Whoever puts himself in tune with It has the mantle of God upon his shoulders.

The ECK Satsang Discourses, **Fourth Series, lesson 4**

The ECK employs Its channels at the place of need, without regard to age, health, location, or any other limitations. It uses every circumstance to reach people with the Light and Sound. The Holy Spirit serves us, and we serve It.

Autobiography of a Modern Prophet, **chap. 38**

Service means that every move, every thought, everything we do gets the best advantage. No matter what thought we have or what action we take, it results in the most productive deed that we can do as Soul learning to become a Co-worker with God. I have often referred to this service as the Law of Economy. It means that in every way we look for the best. We look to excel in every way. If we are going to paint a picture, it will be the best we can do today. Yet tomorrow we will be able to do it better. If we write a book today, it's going to be great; but the book we write tomorrow will be even better. We use the Law of Economy: Only as many words as we need, and that's all.

In every way we look for the best. We look to excel in every way.

How to Find God, **Mahanta Transcripts, Book 2, chap. 22**

Many of the foods I like make it difficult to talk. If I didn't have any talks to give, I'd eat whatever I wanted. But when you serve the ECK, you find out how to change your diet to get the most out of your body. This is working with the Law of Economy.

Cloak of Consciousness, **Mahanta Transcripts, Book 5, chap. 16**

The Wayshower teaches . . . survival to his students in spiritual things. His simple methods are usually overlooked as he arranges the chela's karmic debts into some semblance of order. Karma due for repayment is fed back to his charges in accord with the Law of Economy.

The Living Word, **Book 1, chap. 12**

The Law of Economy makes an accommodation for every area of one's development: physical, psychic, mental, and spiritual.

The ECK Satsang Discourses, **Fourth Series, lesson 10**

With the Law of Economy . . . you get what you need. As a child you don't have many choices. As you grow older, you should have more. We look for spiritual freedom, and this also means we must have freedom of choice. The further we go along the path of ECK and the higher we go into the worlds of God, the more choice we expect to have. . . .

The spiritual principle is that you get the most effect out of everything you do, and everything is turned to a spiritual effect. Through doing the spiritual exercises, the forces are no longer being scattered all over and wasted; they are now aligned in one direction, and that direction is home to God, to the Sugmad. So you see that the Law of Economy is important. What usually isn't noticed is that the Law of Economy is expressed in everything we do and in the people we meet every day.

The Secret Teachings, **Mahanta Transcripts, Book 3, chap. 17**

The spiritual principle is that you get the most effect out of everything you do, and everything is turned to a spiritual effect.

When something isn't carried out the way I'd like, the first thing I do is ask, Where's my responsibility in this? Is it possible I didn't communicate this clearly enough? Very often this is true. Working as we do at all the different levels, and with all the different languages we speak, communicating with each other can be quite difficult. As we go higher in ECK, our communication with Spirit becomes clearer. And hopefully, as we go further along the path, the communication among initiates should be cleaner and clearer.

An aspect of the Law of Economy is recognizing the weaknesses in any system on earth. This includes recognizing the weaknesses in our own character and makeup and working with them, as well as recognizing the same traits in other people and trying to work with them.

The Secret Teachings, Mahanta Transcripts, Book 3, chap. 17

We know that the world economy hasn't been operating on the Law of Economy. America is one of the great offenders. How long can you run without paying your debts? Some governments feel they can always start up the presses and print more money. There is a law against people doing this in their basement, but this is how many national governments operate—because they don't realize how the Law of Karma works.

The life of a country spans many decades, and karma doesn't necessarily come back tomorrow morning; it sometimes takes several years. In the meantime, everybody thinks they are getting a free ride. But they are forgetting the basic Law of Economy, which is the Law of Cause and Effect. You pay for everything you get, both spiritually and materially.

Within each lesson is hidden the seed of truth which is needed for you to take the step that follows.

The different countries of the world act like many human beings. They simply don't understand the laws. The ECKist is among the chosen and enlightened who understands, at least in his head if not in practice, that sometime he must pay his debt—if not sooner, then later.

The Secret Teachings, Mahanta Transcripts, Book 3, chap. 17

Take your share of drubbings, because within each lesson is hidden the seed of truth which is needed for you to take the step that follows. But you can't take the next step until you take the step that is right here. You must begin where you are now. When you can live your life fully, under the Law of Economy and the Law of Love, you will be qualified to take the next step.

The Golden Heart, **Mahanta Transcripts,
Book 4, chap. 8**

Knowing how to move in the grace of ECK touches upon the Law of Economy.

Those who pay lip service to the spiritual exercises by giving them a cursory trial complain that ECK does not work for them. Therefore, something is wrong with the program. True to the mold of the loser, failure in their life is always the fault of somebody else. They seldom take responsibility for what they do, and what they do is done in a halfhearted and sloppy way. This is the reason that businessmen today can be the leaders in the spiritual things—because the good ones carry out the Law of Economy for their survival and success.

The ECK Satsang Discourses, **Fourth Series, lesson 2**

If something comes in a more attractive container, we're willing to pay more for it than its real value. Why? Because we like to think we're getting more. In so doing, however, we are not using our resources to the fullest, which is part of the Law of Economy.

Cloak of Consciousness, **Mahanta Transcripts,
Book 5, chap. 10**

Some messages just make good sense. "When you go out to buy, don't show your silver." That's the Law of Economy. A good spiritual reminder is this

You must begin where you are now. When you can live your life fully, under the Law of Economy and the Law of Love, you will be qualified to take the next step.

one, which demonstrates the returns of love: "If you continually give, you will continually have."

The Living Word, Book 1, chap. 27

We can kid ourselves all we want, but the spiritual law is that we have to pay, in some way, for everything we get. This comes under the Law of Economy, which operates in the lower worlds up to the Mental Plane. Higher laws, such as the Law of Love, prevail in the spiritual worlds, but down here we are in the worlds of dichotomies—lack or plenty, highs and lows, riches and poverty.

Karma and reincarnation come under the Law of Economy. If you direct your spiritual energies in the most straightforward way, always keeping in mind where you are going, you will get through these rebirths faster than if you get sidetracked.

You pick a goal, such as God-Realization. Then you open yourself to the Holy Spirit, the ECK, and make your way directly through life to accomplish the goal. There will be help along the way. You take it as it comes, even though it may not seem to fit into your beliefs up to that time.

The Law of Economy starts down here in the physical.

The Golden Heart, Mahanta Transcripts, Book 4, chap. 8

With a discrimination given by the Inner Master, which is part of the Law of Economy, you learn to put aside the unnecessary and deal only with the tasks worthy of your time and energy.

There is no shortcut unless one considers the Law of Economy, which is to take no more effort than is absolutely required to reach God.

The ECK Satsang Discourses, Fourth Series, lesson 6

With a discrimination given by the Inner Master, which is part of the Law of Economy, you learn to put aside the unnecessary and deal only with the tasks worthy of your time and energy.

Cloak of Consciousness, **Mahanta Transcripts, Book 5, chap. 5**

Above the turmoil that rakes the outer man stands the Mahanta—the Divine One of God. He is the epitome of the Law of Economy in living expression; he is the Godman.

The ECK Satsang Discourses, **Fourth Series, lesson 2**

As quickly as the Living ECK Master figures out how to surmount a block, that quickly can he go ahead with a new chapter in his book of prophecies.

This process is called the Law of Economy.

To repeat, all the minor laws of Spirit fall under the grand law: Soul exists because God loves It. All things bring one to the greater glory of Sugmad.

The Law of Economy, then, works whether anyone knows of it or not. The spiritual bumbler is always at odds with it, and he has a host of personal problems for which he finds no relief. Bad habits lock him into the same behavior that brought trouble in the first place, and so the cycle of trouble goes on.

The Law of Economy is an aspect of the ECK. It is always right, clean, and just. There is no pettiness in it, or spite or hatred.

The ECK Satsang Discourses, **Fourth Series, lesson 4**

The Law of Economy is an aspect of the ECK. It is always right, clean, and just. There is no pettiness in it, or spite or hatred.

The ECK Adept knows the Law of Economy. Therefore, his unfoldment is light-years ahead of the average person, and the gap between them grows at a faster rate than the speed of light.

The ECK Satsang Discourses, **Fourth Series, lesson 5**

The Law of Economy presupposes that everything we do is in harmony with ECK, in harmony with life.

The Secret Teachings, **Mahanta Transcripts, Book 3, chap. 17**

The Law of Economy presupposes that everything we do is in harmony with ECK, in harmony with life.

We should always be interested in how we can serve life. Another way to say this is, how can you make things smoother and easier for those people around you? How do you make things go just a little bit better?

This is all that serving life is. You do a little here and a little there, and things get better.

Wisdom from the Master on Spiritual Leadership: ECK Leader's Guide, **article 1**

Facsimiles

Facsimiles, Law of. The sixth law of the physical universe, that all effects in life are brought about by the thoughts and pictures in the mind of the individual.

A Cosmic Sea of Words: The ECKANKAR Lexicon

Facsimiles deal with those pictures you took in the mind. These pictures have been with you since you came into the world. They are filed away by Soul like cards in a little niche in the Soul's body. . . . Generally, facsimiles are either borrowed or they are one's own. One can have either or both through a compulsive basis or on an unknowing basis. They will influence him in one way or another. . . .

These facsimiles are merely little units of energy which gather about the body, mind, and Soul. They keep the attention of the individual "I" on them, especially if they are bothersome pictures. This is what oriental religion keeps calling karma.

The Flute of God, chap. 7

The flows of energy which are recorded in facsimiles are dead flows. In order for them to have any power or life, a new flow of attention must be played over them by the individual. So you see that no matter what is wrong with the individual, he is the one who is keeping it that way. This comes in with cause and effect. When one is on a low level, he fails in his beingness. He is existing on death

All effects in life are brought about by the thoughts and pictures in the mind of the individual.

When an individual is cause he is being positive; when he is effect he is being negative.

wishes, with qualities of unbeingness. The chief aspects of cause and effect are the positive and negative. When an individual is cause he is being positive; when he is effect he is being negative. The art of good picturization is the art of full beingness.

The Flute of God, chap. 7

Secondary sources, to us, refer to people who claim someone else's experiences as their truth. They live by facsimile. This type of experience is secondhand and breeds blind faith.

The difference between a primary and a secondary source is the difference between knowing and faith. In ECK, we want to know what life is all about via our own personal experience here on the physical plane, as well as in the inner worlds.

The Book of ECK Parables, Volume 2, parable 56

Invisible Laws

Invisible Laws. Seven principles of consciousness—appreciation, sincerity, unselfishness, idealism, devotion, personal effort, and attainment.

A Cosmic Sea of Words: The ECKANKAR Lexicon

The seven principles of consciousness . . . are as follows: 1. Appreciation, 2. Sincerity, 3. Unselfishness, 4. Idealism, 5. Devotion, 6. Personal effort, and 7. Attainment.

These are the invisible laws. . . . For example— 1. Appreciation is—appreciation of the teacher; 2. Sincerity is—to inspire the seeker to seek higher levels of consciousness; 3. Unselfishness—the willingness to sacrifice the individual self to the universe; 4. Idealism—the faculty of perceiving spiritual values through a perfect pattern; 5. Devotion—to fill the mind and Soul with love, aspiration and giving of the self to universal consciousness; 6. Personal effort—spiritual motivating force of intelligence which is within all men; 7. Attainment— the reward for spirit action.

Dialogues with the Master, **chap. 36**

Seven principles of consciousness —appreciation, sincerity, unselfishness, idealism, devotion, personal effort, and attainment.

Karma

Karma, Law of. The Law of Cause and Effect, action and reaction, justice, retribution, and reward, which applies to the lower or psychic worlds: the Physical, Astral, Causal, Mental, and Etheric Planes; the Law of Universal Compensation which is under the Law of Vibration; inflow and outflow; a matter of vibrations; one of the twelve laws by which the universes are sustained.

A Cosmic Sea of Words: The ECKANKAR Lexicon

The Law of Karma, yet another facet of the Law of Love, purifies people by holding them responsible for their thoughts and deeds, both to themselves and others.

Wisdom of the Heart, **Book 1, Wisdom Note 8**

In the lower worlds, the Law of Cause and Effect, the Law of Karma, is in force. You must know how to live under it. The Law of Cause and Effect and the experiences that derive from your understanding—or lack of understanding—of that law also bring you to a realization or an acceptance of divine love.

I'm going to give you an idea of how to reestablish your relationship with ECK, beginning with the very fundamental question of what is right and what is wrong.

First, we have to look at cause and effect. Then you can go to the next level, which is understanding your relationship with ECK and finding God's love. Until you know, or have a rule for yourself, of what

The Law of Karma, yet another facet of the Law of Love, purifies people by holding them responsible for their thoughts and deeds, both to themselves and others.

is right and what is wrong, you're going to find yourself having unnecessary problems in any path you take to God.

Wisdom of the Heart, **Book 2, Wisdom Note 7**

The universality of the Law of Karma is one of the chief factors which binds life together, and not only human life but animal, plant, and mineral life as well. All those compose one big family, with a complicated and inseparable history and an inseparable karma.

The Shariyat-Ki-Sugmad, **Book One, chap. 7**

By and large, the Lord of Karma—not the individual—is responsible for selecting the family through which Soul enters the physical plane. Like a guardian who administers a trust on behalf of an infant, he arranges for Soul to join a family which offers the best prospect for spiritual unfoldment. In making that selection, he is under no obligation to consider the feelings or imagined rights of the person so involved. Placement is a simple matter: The Law of Karma, which governs such stationing, is the law. It must be obeyed.

Autobiography of a Modern Prophet, **chap. 3**

Destiny controls the conditions at birth. Much of what an individual does after that is an exercise of free will.

Destiny controls the conditions at birth. Much of what an individual does after that is an exercise of free will. Free will may overcome the conditions of destiny, but first one must awaken his creative talents, through which he can then reshape his spiritual and material life.

To sum up, fate governs the conditions at a person's birth; free will allows a choice as to how he will move within and beyond them.

Autobiography of a Modern Prophet, **chap. 3**

There simply is no such thing as righteous anger. The ECK doesn't recognize any distinctions between anger for a cause and anger for no cause. Through the Law of Karma, the ECK impartially doles out justice whenever there is any imbalance of the emotions.

The Golden Heart, **Mahanta Transcripts, Book 4, chap. 11**

There simply is no such thing as righteous anger.

When someone wants to be a healer and then takes on another's illness, this karma from the other person was earned. It is often because the individual did not know the laws of Spirit, or perhaps was under the control of one of the five passions of the mind: greed, anger, lust, attachment, and vanity. This is what causes our karma.

Journey of Soul, **Mahanta Transcripts, Book 1, chap. 8**

People who practice psychic healing may get away with it for years, because the Law of Karma is in no hurry. Spirit has plenty of time; It's in no hurry to collect the debt that a man has created. A psychic healer may be very good for ten, twenty, even forty years; but then his health all of a sudden may go bad. The karma has come home; it must be paid. He doesn't know what happened, only that he can heal others but not himself. Furthermore, he doesn't know why it happened. He has absolutely no understanding that he violated the laws of Spirit.

How to Find God, **Mahanta Transcripts, Book 2, chap. 4**

The greater you become in your state of consciousness, the quicker your acts come back to you. In the Bible, St. Paul spoke of this Law of Karma when he said, "Whatsoever a man soweth, that shall he also reap."

How to Find God, **Mahanta Transcripts, Book 2, chap. 2**

As you move along the spiritual path, the higher you go, the quicker it comes back.

Until you come onto the spiritual path, you generally have a lifetime or two behind you that you're paying off, so you can't make the connection between what you did wrong in the past and the payment that is now coming due. As you move along the spiritual path, the higher you go, the quicker it comes back. If you do something that stands between another person and God-Realization, you very quickly find out that you have broken a spiritual law. It comes back sometimes within a week, a few minutes, or even seconds. It comes quickly enough so that you know: Ah! This pain is the result of a lack of understanding of that spiritual law.

How to Find God, **Mahanta Transcripts, Book 2, chap. 4**

When one has not attained the high states of spiritual consciousness, this Law of Karma does not come back immediately. The higher you go in your awareness, the quicker the law comes back. That's good in one way and bad in another. I'd say overall it's good because as soon as you cheat someone, for instance, the law strikes and you get the karma over with sooner. The higher you go, the narrower becomes the path—some call it the razor's edge.

People who do not really have any regard for the spiritual law may just be learning life, taking it as they find it, cheating, robbing, and having a good time. The law does not demand its payment sometimes for two, ten, twenty, or thirty years, or maybe not until the next lifetime. When the payment doesn't come due as soon as the violation of the spiritual law is committed, the person thinks he's getting away scot-free. But there must be full payment in the true coin for every action.

How to Find God, **Mahanta Transcripts, Book 2, chap. 10**

I can help you with some of the burdens, but I won't take them all from you. A debt to God that has been created must be repaid by the one who incurred the debt. This is the Law of Life: Whatsoever a man sows, that also shall he reap.

How to Find God, **Mahanta Transcripts, Book 2, chap. 11**

One of the benefits of the path of ECK is that much of our karma can be worked off on the inner planes so that we don't have to go through it here. If we've created debts, they must be repaid to God. But on the path of ECK we have this advantage: They do not always have to be worked out here on the physical; they can be worked off on the inner planes in the dream state.

How to Find God, **Mahanta Transcripts, Book 2, chap. 12**

One of the benefits of the path of ECK is that much of our karma can be worked off on the inner planes so that we don't have to go through it here.

We have been spoon-fed with ideas of a God who will heal us no matter what we do wrong. Some people think all they have to do is ask. They feel they can give advice to others that might destroy their lives, and by saying, God, please forgive me, it will all be forgotten. Unfortunately these people are ignorant of the spiritual law. St. Paul said, "Whatsoever a man soweth, that shall he also reap," and it means just that. You can kid yourself. A person can eat wrong until it affects his health and then reason that he can always find a doctor who will take care of him. Or he may ask God for a healing. And if it doesn't work he thinks, God didn't heal me; therefore, the God of this faith must not be right. In truth he has incurred a debt to Spirit; he himself must pay it back. No one can help him except himself.

How to Find God, **Mahanta Transcripts, Book 2, chap. 13**

That doctrine of sin . . . waters down the Law of Karma, which holds the doer responsible for each and every deed.

The Master 4 Discourses, **lesson 5**

A person is strong while young, he becomes abusive and power hungry, he controls others. And then this person gets old and loses the power, and younger people come in and have control over this individual.

And never do any of the actors in the play realize that they are playing out the spiritual laws of life, of cause and effect.

The Slow Burning Love of God, **Mahanta Transcripts, Book 13, chap. 8**

For some people, karma comes back the same day. But more often it comes back in a week, two weeks, or a month, so that the person doesn't see the connection. They have no understanding of the Law of Action and Reaction.

The Book of ECK Parables, **Volume 3, parable 58**

An ECK Master simply loves people.

An ECK Master simply loves people.

His divine love reaches out to immature Souls

despite their attacks upon him or ECK initiates under his care. Compassion he has, but also a knowledge that the Law of Karma will teach them better, for all attempts to harm a vehicle of God will, in due course, return upon the sender.

The Master 4 Discourses, **lesson 6**

You make better decisions about what to do or what not to do if you have an understanding of the Law of Cause and Effect.

The Secret of Love, **Mahanta Transcripts, Book 14, chap. 5**

When you don't know the laws of life you break them. And as you break these laws, the Law of Cause and Effect says, "You must pay for them."

The Slow Burning Love of God, **Mahanta Transcripts, Book 13, chap. 3**

The Law of Karma is exact in its measure. To cure a health problem several years in the making often takes a like amount of time for healing. There is no magic way to get an instant, long-term cure without our taking a part in the rebuilding.

A Modern Prophet Answers Your Key Questions about Life, **chap. 5**

There is a time and a place for everything. It is natural for us to chafe against the rules that hinder our freedom. But society puts restraints on us until we learn what consequences we will shoulder for certain actions. Ignorance is no excuse under the Law of Karma.

A Modern Prophet Answers Your Key Questions about Life, **chap. 6**

You make better decisions about what to do or what not to do if you have an understanding of the Law of Cause and Effect.

Spiritual students are held to account for daily karma. If a driver speeds seventy-five miles per hour in a fifty-five-mile-per-hour zone and gets caught, there is a fine to pay. No matter how one tries to fool himself that he is above the Law of Karma, the fine must be paid.

A Modern Prophet Answers Your
Key Questions about Life, **chap. 7**

What makes it so hard to determine right and wrong is that they are only an imperfect mirror image of the spiritual Law of Karma. True, the holy books may give the law in exact terms. Yet when the leaders in politics and religion don't know or understand the full impact of karma, they begin to cut corners, gnawing away at the laws that once insured a strong, peaceful, and fulfilling place for the people.

The Living Word, **Book 2, chap. 17**

Each of us comes to earth with either a mission or a duty.

Each of us comes to earth with either a mission or a duty. Those who have advanced spiritually in past lives and wish now only to serve God, and other living creatures, come with that mission.

Most people, however, still have much to learn about the Law of Cause and Effect, and responsibility. They are very much under the Law of Karma. Their reincarnation is the result of having to fulfill a duty—in other words, bathe in the waters of unknowing and get a lot of experience. Much of it is lost on them. But in the next world after this life, the Lords of Karma review their past life with them and point out what the day-to-day lessons meant to them spiritually.

The Living Word, **Book 2, chap. 32**

Notice how exact the law of return is. The law of Divine Spirit will return your gifts to all areas of need, including even down to the materials needed to build a home in this world or the next.

Letters of Light & Sound 2, **lesson 8**

The Law of Karma is alive and well, as those who try to steal the labors of others discover in the end. There is no hurry to divine law. The Lords of Karma feed out enough rope of opportunity for the "entitled" to bind themselves with all the knots they please, but retribution, or payment, does eventually come due.

Letters of Light & Sound 2, **lesson 1**

The ECK writings tell us of three kinds of karma that affect this life: fate, reserve, and daily. ECK members sometimes forget that the spiritual Law of Cause and Effect remains active throughout their lives on earth, even after reaching the Soul Plane.

The Master 3 Discourses, **lesson 8**

Whether in the dream worlds or here in the physical world, there are always people who believe they can harm others in the name of God. They just don't understand the Law of Retribution. So when their lives go to ruin, they cry to God for help, even as they continue their efforts to harm God's messengers. How could anyone be so blind? Yet people often are.

Wisdom of the Heart, **Book 2, Wisdom Note 4**

The spiritual law is that everything requires payment in the true coin.

The spiritual law is that everything requires payment in the true coin. An extension of that idea is that one who wants to be free spiritually will not encumber himself with debts that he cannot repay.

The Master 3 Discourses, lesson 11

One who wants to be free spiritually will not encumber himself with debts that he cannot repay.

Cause and effect are two necessary threads of life in the lower worlds. Even those of a higher spiritual evolution cannot ignore the Law of Cause and Effect as long as they are in human form.

The Master 3 Discourses, lesson 8

The Law of Karma serves us better in our everyday lives than does the theory of sin. Karma covers all bases.

Letters of Light & Sound 1, lesson 3

During certain periods of history, the bulk of the laws are just. However, when a society drifts from an instinctive sense for the spiritual Law of Karma, which sets the highest standard for right and wrong, then the laws become unjust.

The laws are unjust because the people themselves are unsure about right and wrong. The leaders of such a society merely reflect the spiritual ignorance of the people. A society with poor leadership has only itself to blame.

The Living Word, Book 2, chap. 17

Eckankar can show all people the most direct route home to God.

Yes, there is a quicker exit from the wheel of karma and reincarnation, but most people will settle for a longer, more difficult way home.

What about spiritual freedom? It is Soul's final release from the Law of Karma and Reincarnation.

The Living Word, Book 2, chap. 8

Life on earth is very exacting in the lessons it teaches about the Law of Cause and Effect. It's the old principle of an eye for an eye, and a tooth for a tooth.

Yet life has more to offer than the rigid Law of Karma, which by itself would make life here a miserable existence indeed. Karma is exacting to the letter. All who live under its law (which includes most of humanity) find that everything has a stiff price tag or some other penalty. Yet there is a balance even to the Law of Karma—that of love. In essence, it means that when Divine Spirit sends a blessing of love to us, we must pass it on to someone else or suffer a reversal in spiritual growth.

The Living Word, **Book 2, chap. 22**

The ECK, through the Law of Karma, deals justice impartially to any imbalance of the emotions.

The Book of ECK Parables, **Volume 2, chap. 4**

The spiritual parasites of society may appear to prosper for a while, but in the end, who can hope to frustrate the Law of Karma? It only hurts their spiritual growth until, finally, their deeds catch up with them.

The Law of Karma has a way of calling in spiritual debt for repayment when the debtor is least ready or able to repay it. Yet each is his own victim. Misery and injustice may appear to strike unjustly, but all violations of the Law of Karma come due in good time.

Wisdom of the Heart, **Book 2, Wisdom Note 8**

Karma accounts for those webs and ropes that keep us tied to very old relationships that have

There is a balance even to the Law of Karma—that of love. In essence, it means that when Divine Spirit sends a blessing of love to us, we must pass it on to someone else.

been going on for centuries. We are so tied to others by karma before we come into ECK that we cannot make a move without leaning on someone else.

Once we come into ECK, these bands of karma begin to dissolve, and eventually they drop away. Only then can we stand on our own, with love. Our relationships and associations with other people are no longer based on the Law of Karma which says you are thrown together because you have to resolve this or that. Now we have the freedom to choose the people we want around us.

Once we come into ECK, these bands of karma begin to dissolve, and eventually they drop away.

Unlocking the Puzzle Box, **Mahanta Transcripts, Book 6, chap. 12**

People who do psychic healings are often plagued by karmic overload. They don't know how to be detached about it. They get so emotional about the health of their patients that they find themselves constantly ill.

It happens simply because they do not recognize or understand the Law of Karma. They don't realize that the people who come to them for a healing have earned those illnesses through violation of some spiritual law.

The Eternal Dreamer, **Mahanta Transcripts, Book 7, chap. 9**

Things move very rapidly once an individual comes into Eckankar. Sometimes it seems as if the Law of Karma speeds up. But rather than a speeding up of karma, the experience is more a by-product of expanded awareness.

The Eternal Dreamer, **Mahanta Transcripts, Book 7, chap. 13**

The Law of Karma works in a certain way for most people who are not in ECK. A curtain stands between cause and effect. In ECK, very soon after you do something that hinders you or someone else spiritually, the curtain is pulled up and the deed comes right back at you. It happens quickly enough to be within reach of your memory so that you can learn from it. Sometimes the act comes back so fast that the only way to miss the lesson would be to develop total amnesia.

In other teachings, where the Light and Sound of God is not as direct, the curtain between cause and effect stays down much longer.

The Dream Master, **Mahanta Transcripts, Book 8, chap. 6**

We are responsible for whatever we do. According to the Law of Karma, any act we perform sets something in motion.

The Drumbeat of Time, **Mahanta Transcripts, Book 10, chap. 2**

We are responsible for whatever we do.

Rules passed on to us by our parents, church leaders, and political leaders are not going to make us better spiritual beings. That is trying to impose outer rules on Soul, which works by an entirely different set of guidelines. Soul works by other rules—rules that sometimes the human consciousness isn't aware of.

One of these rules is: You pay for everything you get.

This is the Law of Karma.

What Is Spiritual Freedom? **Mahanta Transcripts, Book 11, chap. 2**

Each time you move from the circle of the home to the circle of school or business, you are entering a whole new world. There you will run into people who are working out their problems. While they are working out their problems, you are also working out your own.

This is how the Law of Karma works in everyday living. The end result is that we are to become people of love and compassion who allow other people to be themselves.

What Is Spiritual Freedom? **Mahanta Transcripts, Book 11, chap. 6**

How do we treat God's creatures? How do we treat other people? How do we treat ourselves? How do we act? How do we think? The law of life known as the Law of Karma is the great teacher. As you sow, so shall ye reap. It's not a vindictive law; it's a law designed to open the heart to love and understanding.

How the Inner Master Works, **Mahanta Transcripts, Book 12, chap. 10**

As you sow, so shall ye reap. It's not a vindictive law; it's a law designed to open the heart to love and understanding.

Eventually they'll learn that the law of life is exacting, returning to each person exactly what that person gives to life. This we call the Law of Karma.

How the Inner Master Works, **Mahanta Transcripts, Book 12, chap. 8**

According to the Law of Karma, if I'm not willing to allow another the freedom to come and go, then I lose my freedom to come and go.

The Slow Burning Love of God, **Mahanta Transcripts, Book 13, chap. 3**

There are purgatories where people go for a time between lifetimes where they work out some of the more overt problems they have caused by breaking the Law of Karma. But these aren't eternal. Soul is eternal, and purgatory belongs to the lower worlds, which are perishable.

The Slow Burning Love of God, **Mahanta Transcripts, Book 13, chap. 6**

When trouble comes, realize that you ultimately have created that problem for yourself, according to the Law of Karma, the Law of Cause and Effect. You created this problem for yourself because of a lack of knowledge in the ways of divine law.

The Slow Burning Love of God, **Mahanta Transcripts, Book 13, chap. 3**

Life will always teach you better.

Life will always teach you better. This is the basis of the Law of Karma: what you sow, you reap. And in the reaping of what we've sown, we gain spiritual wisdom.

How to Survive Spiritually in Our Times, **Mahanta Transcripts, Book 16, chap. 4**

Each person must answer for all deeds, for he knows the Law of Karma requires him to balance the accounts of Soul.

The Easy Way Discourses, **lesson 4**

An ECKist who is aware of the exact nature of the Law of Karma can sidestep the shadow of envy that often engulfs those who do not understand the sudden good fortune of others. All is in its rightful place. Everything is at the exact station it deserves in life, so he can get on with his own unfoldment and keep a cheerful spirit.

The Easy Way Discourses, **lesson 4**

There is little respect for life in today's highly mechanized food chain, so it's hardly surprising that the Law of Karma acts to return this lack of respect to the consumer—in the form of sickness and disease.

The Master 4 Discourses, **lesson 10**

The Law of Karma is only a textbook of Divine Spirit to teach immature Souls about the laws of God. Once an individual grasps the spiritual laws, he has the secret of life.

The Master 4 Discourses, **lesson 9**

Even some of the most broad-minded people— we find them as leaders in religion and politics—don't understand the Law of Cause and Effect. What are the causes that drive life here? What are the responsibilities that a Soul has in this life? If our leaders understood the spiritual Law of Cause and Effect, they would be making entirely different decisions, especially if they knew they are accountable for their actions in government.

The Secret of Love, **Mahanta Transcripts, Book 14, chap. 5**

You'll see things; you'll gain wisdom. Sometimes you go to Temples of Golden Wisdom. Sometimes an ECK Master will be teaching you in the dream state.

You'll see things; you'll gain wisdom. Sometimes you go to Temples of Golden Wisdom. Sometimes an ECK Master will be teaching you in the dream state, giving you spiritual exercises. These exercises can help you travel further into the dream worlds or get deeper insights into the secret laws of life.

In other words, you may get a better understanding of the Law of Cause and Effect—not the fact that it exists, but how it works in your everyday life. It helps you.

The Slow Burning Love of God, **Mahanta Transcripts,
Book 13, chap. 9**

There is no line that says, "This is where responsibility ends and freedom begins." There is no such line; you have to decide that for yourself. And according to the Law of Cause and Effect, experience will teach you if your decision was good or not.

The Slow Burning Love of God, **Mahanta Transcripts,
Book 13, chap. 3**

The Law of Cause and Effect is, on one side, a training school, where we learn the lessons that life has to teach. If you want something of great value, you're going to have to work hard for it. There's no free lunch; there is no easy street.

When you learn the lessons, when you understand the Law of Cause and Effect, you graduate to the realization of divine love. Your life becomes richer in the blink of an eye, because you have moved from the consciousness of the masses to the spiritual consciousness of God, of divine love.

The Slow Burning Love of God, **Mahanta Transcripts,
Book 13, chap. 1**

When you learn the lessons, when you understand the Law of Cause and Effect, you graduate to the realization of divine love.

Everyone thinks of karma as bad stuff that happens to you for the bad stuff you did. But karma is the good and the bad. In other words it's cause and effect, anything that occurs.

If you want something from life, you must first earn it.

The Slow Burning Love of God, **Mahanta Transcripts,
Book 13, chap. 1**

Whoever breaks the law must pay the price. In ECK, we know this is how spiritual law works.

Letters of Light & Sound 1, lesson 3

At times when I speak about the basic values, the basic moral codes, some initiates get very upset. If I speak about the Law of Karma as it applies to people trying to get something for nothing, they all agree with me in principle. But at a past ECK seminar, I applied it to social programs. And boy, was there a lot of heat coming from Higher Initiates. The Law of Karma is true, they said, but let's not knock the social programs. Let's not defame the government's attempt to make life easier for everybody. All of a sudden they feel the Law of Karma does not apply, that cause and effect no longer works if it threatens our entitlements.

If you're going to get some-thing out of life, you're going to have to put in an equal amount of effort.

Basic cause and effect means: If someone promises to give you something and delivers it, you'll have to pay for it; you'll have to give something up. If someone is promising to give you a whole lot, that's going to cost you a whole lot. What are you willing to give up? That's the Law of Cause and Effect.

If you're going to get something out of life, you're going to have to put in an equal amount of effort. And if you don't give to life, you won't get back from life. You won't, you can't. It's absolutely impossible.

Wisdom from the Master on Spiritual Leadership:
ECK Leader's Guide, article 64

Nature

laws of nature.   The laws of the negative power; the laws of the physical universe; the natural laws.

A Cosmic Sea of Words: The ECKANKAR Lexicon

While on Earth man is subject to the laws of the negative power, or what are often termed "The Laws of Nature."

Dialogues with the Master, chap. 29

The Law of Nature tells us little or practically nothing about nature but certainly something about man. Assertions about the world are really assertions about ourselves. What man experiences in the ordinary course of life relatively is nothing but the Absolute experienced in a special way.

Dialogues with the Master, chap. 37

Now the law of the world as we know it is this: If a man's attention is focused upon an object which gives him pleasure, he will have pain if it is removed.

So you see, this law of nature compels us to place the attention of many on a permanent object so that there will not be an unbalancing of the emotions too greatly through pleasure or pain.

Dialogues with the Master, chap. 13

To understand ourselves and our place in the world, we might pay more attention to the natural

Assertions about the world are really assertions about ourselves. What man experiences in the ordinary course of life relatively is nothing but the Absolute experienced in a special way.

laws, to the life cycles of animals and plants.

The Dream Master, **Mahanta Transcripts,**
Book 8, chap. 10

If we wish to understand what is to be and what is right, we simply study the laws of nature. Nature shows how truth has manifested itself in the past.

The Dream Master, **Mahanta Transcripts,**
Book 8, chap. 10

The laws of nature can be bent when there is a need for protection or for a spiritual lesson. Usually the experience is given as a way for an individual to learn something that could not be learned any other way. He is raised to a higher state of consciousness much in the same way as when he travels to a Temple of Golden Wisdom.

Unlocking the Puzzle Box, **Mahanta Transcripts,**
Book 6, chap. 13

The law of nature usually sees change occur gradually.

The ECK Satsang Discourses, **Fourth Series, lesson 12**

Nature reflects the laws of ECK. Therefore, observe its workings in the habits of birds, the cycles of plants, and the instincts of reptiles and mammals. All sing the glory of ECK; all teach the secrets of life.

Nature reflects the laws of ECK. Therefore, observe its workings in the habits of birds, the cycles of plants, and the instincts of reptiles and mammals. All sing the glory of ECK; all teach the secrets of life. Watch the coming and going of clouds, the waxing and waning of the moon, and the rising and setting of the sun. They reveal the natural order of creation. Everything is right when there is neither too much nor too little for the time and place. So is it also with your spiritual life.

Wisdom of the Heart, **Book 1, Wisdom Note 10**

Polarity

Polarity, Law of. The Law of Opposites. The third law of the physical universe; the state of opposition between any two related factors; yin and yang (negative and positive), feminine and masculine; the negative, or reactive, side and the positive, or active, side; the third part is the passive, or middle, path; each thing within this universe is supported, animated, maintained by, and is in opposition to its opposite.

A Cosmic Sea of Words: The ECKANKAR Lexicon

Polarity simply means the state of opposition between any two related factors: light and darkness, heat and cold, material and immaterial, harmony and discord, positive and negative, north and south, male and female, etc.

The Flute of God, **chap. 7**

Polarity simply means the state of opposition between any two related factors.

This law states that every phenomenon, on whatever scale and in whatever world it may take place, from molecular to cosmic phenomena, is the result of combining the meeting of the two, plus the third, which is the passive middle. This is not the passive element that you find in negation, but a balancing of the two. It is the path which Buddha called the "Middle Path.". . . Scientific thought today realizes the existence of positive and negative forces. . . . But science has never raised the question of a third force. According to exact divine science, one force, or two forces, can never produce

121

phenomenon. The presence of the third is always necessary to produce any phenomenon. This neutral force is not easily accessible to direct observation and understanding.

The idea of the unity of the three in Absolute ECK forms the basis of the three worlds and of the ancient teachings.

The Flute of God, chap. 7

Within this material universe the Law of Polarity, or the Law of Opposites, operates. Nothing exists except in relation to its opposite. This is also true within the psychic worlds: Astral, Causal, and Mental.

Within this material universe the Law of Polarity, or the Law of Opposites, operates. Nothing exists except in relation to its opposite. This is also true within the psychic worlds: Astral, Causal, and Mental. However, within the heavenly worlds this is not true; for here it is true that there are no opposites, although the sacred scriptures of the worlds say so.

These scriptures claim that the good go into some heavenly paradise while the evil will be punished forever in some fiery region. This is the Law of the Opposites, or Polarity. Those who are good attract the good, and those who are evil attract the evil. Therefore, in the heavenly states, it's found that polarity or chemistry within two objects no longer exists, and that Soul is free to do whatever It desires as long as it falls within a general pattern of the heavenly law. This law is: Love is all, and do as thou wilt.

The Shariyat-Ki-Sugmad, Book Two, chap. 7

Anyone who lives on this side of the Law of Polarity is not free, but is one who is always reacting to circumstances, who is enslaved to reactive habits, who is always being exploited, and is desirous of materialistic factors. . . .

When one gains perfect knowledge of the Spirit, he does not have to give up the physical body and subtle bodies at once. He has his choice of going on living here as long as he is in perfect harmony with Spirit as Its agent and is not bothered with the Law of the Opposites.

The Flute of God, chap. 7

One of these laws is: "Nothing can exist except in relation to its opposite." This is an age-old principle of the positive and negative. The positive is the outgoing, the God force; and the negative is the inert, receptive force.

For example, laughter must have its opposite, tears; and neither can the universe have complete joy without sorrow. Therefore, this universe is not static, but is a constant dynamic state. There is nothing eternal on this plane but change itself. This is where God arrives in our lives, for behind the change lies the eternal, the unchanging which the outer eye cannot see. As long as anything exists on the mental and physical plane, it is due to be in constant change.

Now, the second principle is, "That the positive is forever transforming into the negative and correspondingly, the negative is forever in the process of becoming the positive.". . .

Each power needs the other in this world. Without one the other could not exist. . . . The teachings need to be revitalized and reformed to show the world how to take advantage of the two forces, not to put a strain upon the individual aspirant to hold to one constantly, when it is almost an impossibility unless he is trained by the ECK Master. Therefore, do not despair if the cycle strikes in a low depression at one time, and then later turns to the higher, and vice versa.

Dialogues with the Master, chap. 8

This universe is not static, but is a constant dynamic state. There is nothing eternal on this plane but change itself. This is where God arrives in our lives, for behind the change lies the eternal.

Beyond the Soul Plane in those worlds of Spirit, we begin to work in the whole. There are no regions or planes that we know of; it is simply one world of Light. In the lower regions where we exist now, something can be known only by its counterpart—truth by untruth, light by darkness. At the Soul Plane as this ECK Stream, or Spirit of God, comes down from the God center, It splits into two parts: the positive and the negative. We have manifestations of this split, and though we take it for granted, it shows up all around us. If you want to iron, you first put the plug into the wall outlet, and this uses alternating currents—the positive and the negative. We see the height of the mountains and the depths of the valleys, because the only way anything can be known in these lower worlds is in comparison to its opposite. We're always thinking in parts.

The Greek philosophers came close to having the spiritual viewpoint. They tried to have an overview when they looked at life as it existed here, and they would address it from the whole. In the West, we fragment it—man and woman, happiness and sadness—and generally view life in its parts.

The ECKist is a realist, for he knows how to use the Law of Polarity.

How to Find God, Mahanta Transcripts, Book 2, chap. 12

When Soul enters into the regions of immortality, or worlds of true Spirit above the psychic worlds, It finds no opposites. Light is light and there is no opposite to it and the sounds of ECK, only the polarity of the highest qualities. Therefore, the ECKist is a realist, for he knows how to use the Law of Polarity. When he has to use his consciousness in the psychic world, he is able to take advantage of the Law of Opposites. But when he is in the

world of the true Kingdom of God, then he is able
to use the Law of Polarity for his own benefit through
this conscious state.

The Shariyat-Ki-Sugmad, Book Two, chap. 7

Progression
(Unfoldment)

Progression (or Unfoldment), Law of. Soul is inevitably bound to become a Co-worker with God. It means going through all the steps that lead to this. To teach Soul how to give and receive divine love.

A Cosmic Sea of Words: The ECKANKAR Lexicon

The Law of Unfoldment, or Progression, in the lower worlds always operates under the great Law of Love, which is the entirety of the Holy ECK that permeates and gives sustenance to all creation.

The ECK Satsang Discourses, **Fourth Series, lesson 10**

Spiritual unfoldment never stops; it goes on and on. No matter how far you have come today, you can go further tomorrow. And no matter how far you come in this lifetime, of necessity you must go much further in your next lifetime. Spiritual law requires that you go either forward or backward.

Spiritual unfoldment never stops; it goes on and on.

How the Inner Master Works, **Mahanta Transcripts, Book 12, chap. 6**

The Law of Progression is linked to another grand law at the top of the lower planes: the Law of Economy.

The ECK Satsang Discourses, **Fourth Series, lesson 10**

The Law of Unfoldment, then, is to teach Soul how to give and receive divine love.

The Law of Unfoldment, then, is to teach Soul how to give and receive divine love.

The ECK Satsang Discourses, **Fourth Series, lesson 10**

Since Soul entered this earthly theater, It has been both the perpetrator and victim of an endless array of horrors. Each person who is alive today has been in either of the two roles times without number, testing the limits of the hidden spiritual laws that prohibit one individual from imposing upon another any limits to Soul's right to unfold in consciousness.

The ECK Satsang Discourses, **Third Series, lesson 7**

The law of the universe is that each person has the right to choose his own course of progress on earth.

The ECK Satsang Discourses, **Fourth Series, lesson 3**

Protection

Spiritual Protection, Law of. Follows the principle of "Speak not; harm not those who are the bearers of Light, for harm will come to him who does." The Mahanta, the Living ECK Master offers spiritual protection to all followers of ECK.

A Cosmic Sea of Words: The ECKANKAR Lexicon

The old Law of Protection is this: "Nothing can hurt us unless we ourselves allow it!"

The Living Word, **Book 1, chap. 21**

A person always has free will. Even the Mahanta cannot give anyone protection unless that person allows him to do so, because that is the spiritual law.

A Modern Prophet Answers Your Key Questions about Life, **chap. 3**

There are several means of protection that are possible to use against those who intrude into our state of being. One simple method is putting a reversed mirror between yourself and the harm. This is done by imagining a mockup of a mirror that reflects back to the sender all unwanted thoughts and forces.

Another form of self-protection is to put yourself in a white circle of light. Then look out from this center at whatever is disturbing you. You may also imagine a wall that shields you from the psychic enemy.

The Art of Spiritual Dreaming, **chap. 6**

The old Law of Protection is this: "Nothing can hurt us unless we ourselves allow it!"

The ECK Masters are the guardian angels around you all the time.

When we speak of opening your wings, it's coming into an awareness of the spiritual love and protection of the ECK Masters.

They are the guardian angels around you all the time. It's just a matter of opening your awareness and going above the human consciousness to recognize and benefit from this.

The Secret of Love, **Mahanta Transcripts, Book 14, chap. 8**

Resonance

Resonance, Law of. Each initiation opens the gate to certain regions of the corresponding plane and new levels of consciousness.

A Cosmic Sea of Words: The ECKANKAR Lexicon

The Third Initiation opens the gate to your free coming and going to certain regions of the Causal Plane, the region of first causes. This level of consciousness deals with cause and effect, as well as with past lives. Yet as a new Third, you're ready to accept only some of the knowledge that is available with respect to the many interplays of the Law of Resonance in storage there.

The Wisdom Notes, December 2000

Each initiation opens the gate to certain regions of the corresponding plane and new levels of consciousness.

131

Reversed Effort

Reversed Effort, Law of. The functioning of the imagination by negation which draws into the external that which one is trying to avoid.

A Cosmic Sea of Words: The ECKANKAR Lexicon

For example the Law of Reversed Effort is simply that the harder a person struggles to achieve some goal, the more difficulty he will have to overcome; difficulty caused, at least in part, by the strain of his effort. "You try too hard; relax, take it easy, and try again," is an expression we hear so much in the Western world. We must make the mind one-pointed, as the Eastern adepts say, but nothing mental should be strained. We should never try to force results. We should stick to our task and finish out the race, but never knock ourselves out doing it.

ECKANKAR—The Key to Secret Worlds, chap. 9

"You try too hard; relax, take it easy, and try again," is an expression we hear so much.

This is known in ECK as the Law of Reversed Effort! This law is a practical law of nature concerned only with man, for man is the only animal on earth that can make use of his imaginative powers! This law is concerned with the imagination. It goes like this: The more you try to put your imaginative powers upon something in concentrated effort, the less you can do it. The harder one struggles to achieve some goal, the more difficulty he will have to overcome; difficulty caused, at least in part, by the strain of his effort. "You tried too hard, relax, take it easy, and try again," are frequently heard expressions. It means to try not to force results!

Take, for example, when one is trying to ride a bicycle through rocks on a road, trying to avoid hitting the large ones, he is so conscious of hitting the rocks he'll probably do so. Or if a man tries to walk across a small plank from one building to another at the tenth floor, his mind would be on falling and not on the walking. You see this law is concerned with imagining and feeling! What you image must have feeling—therefore the negative imaging is more likely to be effective than the positive imaging because the negative has feeling with it!

Letters to Gail, **Volume I, January 23, 1963**

Any situation, when altered by force, will tend to persist. This is why so many people fail to resolve their problems, no matter who might be helping them.

Of course, any situation, when altered by force, will tend to persist. This is why so many people fail to resolve their problems, no matter who might be helping them. Force will make the problem and situation more solid regardless of whatever resolve there is to change them. Generally, the greater an untruth is in these circumstances, the more solid it will become if force is used.

The Key to ECKANKAR, **p. 37**

The problem with surrender is that the more one tries to give something up, the harder it is to do. It is the Law of Reversed Effort.

Letters of Light & Sound 1, **lesson 10**

Spiritual Growth

Spiritual Growth, Law of. Truth has to be continually rediscovered, reformed, and transformed; the same truth has to be experienced in ever-new forms.

A Cosmic Sea of Words: The ECKANKAR Lexicon

Spiritual law governs when and how a seeker makes the leap from his immature beliefs to those of a higher nature that are very clear about an individual's rights *and* responsibilities as a spiritual being.

The Master 4 Discourses, **lesson 12**

The Law of Growth in the lower worlds demands that everything must go slower and slower as it ages. Finally one settles into a rut, becomes less mobile, until death is the final state. Only the Spiritual Exercises of ECK can renew consciousness and insure Soul an escape from rebirth and death.

Wisdom of the Heart, **Book 1, chap. 11**

Only the Spiritual Exercises of ECK can renew consciousness and insure Soul an escape from rebirth and death.

Truth cannot be taken as one's own discovery, but it has to be continually rediscovered. It has to be reformed and transformed if its meaning, its living value and spiritual nourishment are to be preserved. This is known as the Law of Spiritual Growth, which results in the necessity to experience the same truth in ever-new forms, and to

135

cultivate and propagate not so much the results, but the methods through which Soul obtains knowledge, experience, and reality.

The Shariyat-Ki-Sugmad, Book Two, chap. 10

Unity

Unity, Law of. The seventh law of the physical universe; thinking in the whole instead of the parts.

A Cosmic Sea of Words: The ECKANKAR Lexicon

The seventh law of the physical universe is: the Law of Unity, thinking in the whole instead of in parts. It is a simple way of knowing the solution to the problem the instant it presents itself. In a way this is called liberation from the bondage of the world, which men have always cried to their God to give them.

This law simply means that one must be wholly within the ECK in order to enjoy himself as the whole man and be able to select consciously what he wants in life and work at it.

The Flute of God, **chap. 7**

One must be wholly within the ECK in order to enjoy himself as the whole man and be able to select consciously what he wants in life and work at it.

Some of the ancient Greek philosophers used to think from the whole. They would consider the overview. Western man usually thinks in terms of the parts. Most people think only in fragments; and because they do, they can't step back and take a look at the whole situation, so a problem defeats them before they've taken even one step.

How to Find God, **Mahanta Transcripts, Book 2, chap. 21**

Vibration

Vibrations, Law of.   The fourth law of the physical universe which governs all the influences such as wavelengths, outflows, inflows, cause and effect, and the harmonics of the movement of sound.

A Cosmic Sea of Words: The ECKANKAR Lexicon

The fourth law of this universe is the Law of Vibration, or Harmonics: This is the law that governs all the influences upon the Soul and body in this world, such as wavelengths; outflows from the planets, stars, and heavenly bodies; music; sound; color; and general harmonics. Under this principle falls karma, cause and effect and inflow and outflow.

This is the law that governs all the influences upon the Soul and body in this world.

The Flute of God, **chap. 7**

Close observance shows the manifestation of the Law of Harmonics in vibrations of every kind including light, heat, chemistry, and other vibratory sciences.

The Flute of God, **chap. 7**

From the seven scales of music, each octave, do-re-mi-fa-sol-la-ti, contains a good foundation for understanding the cosmic laws of vibrations. Each octave has an ascending octave, in which frequency of vibrations increase. . . . As one goes along the scale, it is found to descend, after ti, and continue going around the scale again and again, until it

139

makes a circle or something similar to a circle. This is true of the physical universe for nothing keeps a straight line.

The Flute of God, **chap. 7**

*Nothing in the
physical world
stays in the
same place, or
remains what
it was.*

Nothing in the physical world stays in the same place, or remains what it was; everything moves, everything is going somewhere, is changing inevitably, either develops or goes down, weakens or degenerates. . . . Ascent or descent is the inevitable cosmic condition of any action.

The Flute of God, **chap. 7**

Pain and the past are nothing more than love's chrysalis, its shell, its seedbed, in which these necessary nothings release such real wonders, such as the comforting thrill of God's hand on one's shoulder.

Laws of Charity

The laws that bring Soul a greater
capacity to love

Chela, Laws and
Rules for the

Chela, Laws and Rules for the. Give harmony, purity, and perfection of Soul.

A Cosmic Sea of Words: The ECKANKAR Lexicon

The laws and rules for the ECK chela are simple. These are to give harmony, purity, and perfection of Soul. This constitutes heaven while in the physical vehicle.

The Shariyat-Ki-Sugmad, **Book One, chap. 5**

He must practice the disciplines of ECK. The first is to have cleanliness of mind, that no words which would pollute the air enter into his mind. He shall look upon all men as creatures of God and this only; for they, like himself, are temples who shall eventually become Co-workers with God.

He must, in mind, fast continuously from all Kal thoughts which could infect his mental state and consciousness. Through this he learns the powerful awareness of the presence of the Living ECK Master, who is with him constantly. He learns not to be deceived or dismayed by the conflicting world around him. He knows that all universes, regardless of whether or not they are under the rulership of the Kal Niranjan, are really worlds of perfection, harmony, and good.

He learns that patience is the greatest discipline of all the spiritual works of ECK. By patience

The laws and rules for the ECK chela are simple. These are to give harmony, purity, and perfection of Soul.

he can endure life, hardships, karmic burdens, the slanders of men, and the pricks of pain and disease. He keeps his mind steadfastly upon the Light of God, never swerving, never letting up on his attention to the goal of God-Realization.

He comes to know humility and chastity in his life on earth and that all his responsibility belongs to God, not to anyone nor anything within this physical realm. His loved ones, family, and relatives are the images of God, mirrored in this worldly life and embodiment to serve the Sugmad, the Supreme Deity. . . .

He will come to discriminate between all things, that there is no good nor evil, no beauty nor ugliness, and there is no sin. That all these are concepts of the mind, the dual forces in the matter worlds. Once he recognizes and understands this, he will then be free of all the Kal traps.

He will be ready to enter into the Kingdom of God, the Ocean of Love and Mercy.

He will be the ECK, of Itself.

The Shariyat-Ki-Sugmad, Book One, chap. 5

The path of ECK doesn't eliminate the five passions of the mind; we learn how to control them.

The path of ECK doesn't eliminate the five passions of the mind; we learn how to control them. How? By focused attention, the power of Soul, which is ignited by the chanting of your word. By chanting your word, you instantly have the power to raise yourself in consciousness to the point where you are able to step back from any situation so that it doesn't overwhelm you. Then you can look at it objectively and unemotionally, and figure out what's happening. Ask yourself: Is it in my best interest? or Is someone using his creative imagination to trap me within the dimensions of his time and space?

How to Find God, Mahanta Transcripts, Book 2, chap. 18

To live in this truth, to abide in the Word, is to
bear the harvest of all things in the richest manner:
that is, to live harmoniously in the spiritual senses.

The Key to ECKANKAR, **p. 40**

Creativity

Creativity, Law of. Every atom is striving continually to manifest more life; all are intelligent, and all are seeking to carry out the purpose for which they were created.

A Cosmic Sea of Words: The ECKANKAR Lexicon

Life is a mystery until we come to the path of ECK. We begin to understand that we can be the creators of our own world and that, in truth, what we are today is a creation of that which we have made from the past. There is a way to change the future, and we can do it. But you don't do it by wishing.

Life is a mystery until we come to the path of ECK.

When an individual looks for God-Realization, it has to be more than a passing fancy. It's not like a fashion that you only wear for a season; you don't just forget your high aspirations for God. It must be something that is within your heart in a gentle way. You know that no matter what happens on the path, it is always to lead you closer to the source of Soul's creation in the heart of God. Soul wants to return home.

How to Find God, **Mahanta Transcripts, Book 2, chap. 3**

You develop a sense of humor, and as challenges come up, you begin to draw on your creativity. You find solutions that would never have occurred to you before. Life becomes more fun—you actually have a more adventuresome life. You get put into situations you would not have been in before, because you are going one step beyond yourself. And as you get yourself in trouble, you also have help to get out of it, because as you learn to work with your own resources, you are developing self-mastery.

How to Find God, **Mahanta Transcripts,
Book 2, chap. 5**

Shakespeare says a poet's function is to reach to heaven for ideas and bring them down to earth. It is true that thought does not originate with man, but in heaven. Where did Beethoven go to find his Fifth Symphony? Did Jesus originate the Sermon on the Mount? When great poetry and great music inspire you, what is conceived, gestated, and born of that? You can choose between noble and ignoble. You understand poetry and music. Love them, and let them flow into your consciousness. So you see that we all are linked to the sun, moon, and stars. We can lift our consciousness to higher planes and see from above, as if from the masthead of a ship, the past, present, and future, all in a moment, through the eyes of Soul.

The Key to ECKANKAR, **p. 27**

Thought creates form, but it is feeling that gives vitality to thought.

Thought creates form, but it is feeling that gives vitality to thought.

Thought without feeling may be constructive as in some engineering work, but it can never be creative in the work of an artist, or a musician. In all that which originates within itself a new order of causation needs to be recognized, a creation, the intertwined reality of thought and feeling. It is this inseparable union of thought and feeling that distinguishes creative thought from analytical thought and places it in a different category. If one is to utilize a new starting point for carrying on the work of creation, it must be done by assimilating the feeling of the divine ECK into the pattern of one's thought by entering into the stream of the ECK.

The images in the mind from the stream of Spirit have to be generic. The reason is that by its very nature the principle of life must be prolific, tending to multiplicity, and the original thought image must be fundamental to the whole race, not limited to particular individuals. Consequently the image in the stream of the ECK must be an absolute type containing the true essentials for the perfect development of the race, just what Plato meant by archetypal ideas. This is the perfect substance of the thing in thought.

Therefore, it is that our unfolding as centers of creative activity, as exponents of new laws, and through them of new conditions, depends on our realization that divine power is the archetype of consciousness perfection, at once as thought and feeling.

The Flute of God, **chap. 9**

Utilize a new starting point for carrying on the work of creation by assimilating the feeling of the divine ECK into the pattern of one's thought by entering into the stream of the ECK.

Danda, the Righteous Law

danda. *DAHN-dah* Self-discipline; sometimes called the righteous law. It treats the divine rights of people as well as kings; works both ways, neither can trespass upon the other's rights.

A Cosmic Sea of Words: The ECKANKAR Lexicon

Those of you who wish to make the effort can also attain this self-mastery in life. You do not come to the point where you begin to direct or control Spirit, because Spirit will not be controlled or directed. People who try to do this are using the psychic powers, black magic. Instead, you let Spirit flow through you without any blocks or obstacles whatsoever. Eventually you become Its pure vehicle, as an ECK Master; and whatever It wants, you carry it out. When you get a direction on the inner planes, you immediately begin figuring ways to carry it out. Sometimes it may take a while. You pick priorities and begin working on them.

How to Find God, **Mahanta Transcripts, Book 2, chap. 5**

You pick priorities and begin working on them.

A Christian who lives the Law of Righteousness is far superior to a chela who engages in useless arguments with other chelas about whether there is dogma in Eckankar. Even though we are ultimately on a path that is centered upon the inner

153

reality of truth, we do need the outer expression of truth while in a human body.

The Living Word, Book 1, chap. 11

The righteous law is called danda. It treats the divine rights of the people as well as that of kings. When it works both ways, it means that neither can trespass upon the other's rights. To have to write law upon the books and use this as a guide to keep society within the moral standards of life is to bring about disorder in a society. As the human race enters upon its decline in civilized standards, there is, and was, a transfer of the center of government from within man to enacted statutes; in other words, from moral standards deeply embedded in the inner consciousness of people to laws written in books. When the time came that the fundamental danda, the Law of Righteousness, was no longer in the hearts of people but in books, then the decline of civilization set in for society.

It is only the ECK Masters who have witnessed such changes and have tried to lift the human race above the decline of every civilization in the history of mankind.

It is only the ECK Masters who have witnessed such changes and have tried to lift the human race above the decline of every civilization in the history of mankind. The task is hard but since the Golden Age, long since passed, every ECK Master who has spent time upon this earth has gone through the Silver Age, the Copper Age, and others to witness the degenerative changes. Slowly has come the Iron Age, which marks the lowest ebb in individual and social degeneration. It is during this period that modern laws, governments, and social regulations began to appear. Men, supposedly wise in nature, hailed these changes as progress. But it's not true that man has progressed in nature, but has decreased due to the workings of the Kal forces. He usually does not recognize such a negative force and, if he does at all, he scorns it as being nothing in his life.

The Shariyat-Ki-Sugmad, Book Two, chap. 4

When you come to the state of self-mastery, it does not mean that you now have license to live life doing whatever you please. It simply means that now you know and understand the laws of Spirit as they apply to you. You know the things you can do and the things you cannot do. And while you make your way through life with these guidelines, you also are being a vehicle for Spirit.

How to Find God, Mahanta Transcripts, Book 2, chap. 11

Eckankar stands for spiritual freedom—plus all the self-responsibility that goes with it. If we want it, we must also give it.

Wisdom from the Master on Spiritual Leadership: ECK Leader's Guide, article 35

People respect a leader who walks the talk.

Just give people space, responsibility, and respect—and watch them grow spiritually. And as they do, you will too.

Wisdom from the Master on Spiritual Leadership: ECK Leader's Guide, article 35

Eckankar stands for spiritual freedom—plus all the self-responsibility that goes with it.

Dharma

dharma. *DAHR-muh* The Law of Life; the righteousness of life; doing what is right; the code of conduct that sustains the right ethics in life.
A Cosmic Sea of Words: The ECKANKAR Lexicon

One takes for granted before he starts on the path of ECK that he is to become well grounded in the fundamentals of righteousness. He must practice the dharma, the law of life itself, in all aspects of his life. This means doing what one ought to do while an ECK chela. Without doing this he cannot make a start in life.
The Shariyat-Ki-Sugmad, **Book One, chap. 7**

Karma, of course, is bound up with reincarnation. It is separated into two parts: cause and righteousness, which are the basic factors that create karma. It is the disobedience of the Law of Dharma, which is rightness or righteousness, the law of life or what ought to be done, that brings about karma for the individual or groups.
The Shariyat-Ki-Sugmad, **Book Two, chap. 4**

It should always be borne in mind that ignoble thoughts and actions inevitably result in unhappy consequences.
The Key to ECKANKAR, **p. 16**

It should always be borne in mind that ignoble thoughts and actions inevitably result in unhappy consequences.

The negative power, or Satan, is merely an instructor who is in charge of God's earthly schoolroom,

157

the place where Soul gains purification so that It may one day reenter the heavenly states of consciousness and become a Co-worker with God.

You and I—Soul—were created in the heart of God and put in the lower worlds because we simply would not serve others. We were self-serving, enjoying our life on the Soul Plane and other worlds, and we would not give anything in any way. And so we came into the lower worlds.

Many of you write and ask, "What is my mission in life?" Very specifically, it is to become a Co-worker with God. How this breaks down for your particular talents is actually between God and you.

How to Find God, **Mahanta Transcripts, Book 2, chap. 1**

Many of you write and ask, "What is my mission in life?" Very specifically, it is to become a Co-worker with God.

Another point is to live the karmaless life. To act without creating further karma is to do everything in the name of God or in the name of that Inner Master within you. This is a simple way to go through life.

How to Find God, **Mahanta Transcripts, Book 2, chap. 1**

We are interested in learning how to live life fully, not how to contemplate and withdraw, or retreat, from life. By living fully, we get the experience we need to one day become a Co-worker with God. You need every conceivable experience. It's better to go out and do something that you would later find was wrong, than to do nothing. At least you learned something—even if it's only that you would never do it again—and you're smarter than you were before.

How to Find God, **Mahanta Transcripts, Book 2, chap. 5**

There is no easy way to explain the teachings of ECK and the truth contained therein. That understanding has to be an individual undertaking. The most we can do for our family is to ask for their goodwill in letting us study the path of our choice. Give them the same freedom and just enjoy each other as people and as loved ones. Sometimes we're able to work it out, sometimes not.

I really don't like the teachings of ECK to come between members of a family, and I certainly don't recommend anyone take the ECK discourses on the sly, such as through an anonymous post office box. That's being dishonest. In the spiritual life you find you have to be honest. We don't look to ethics as our goal, we look to God-Realization: but as we gain in spiritual unfoldment, our ethics do become greater— more so than on any other path.

How to Find God, **Mahanta Transcripts, Book 2, chap. 7**

All I'm concerned about is that the outer life stays in harmony and balance and that you don't go out there and do strange things all of a sudden—give up your job, take all your savings out of the bank, and go off to an ashram. That is not the spiritual life. The spiritual life is carrying out the duties that we have accepted, such as family and children, and figuring out ways to support them. This is where the challenge of life is today.

How to Find God, **Mahanta Transcripts, Book 2, chap. 9**

One of the spiritual principles that I have learned is that there is always a way, no matter what.

One of the spiritual principles that I have learned is that there is always a way, no matter what. If we have a health, financial, or some other kind of situation—there is always a way out.

How to Find God, **Mahanta Transcripts, Book 2, chap. 11**

A person who wishes to move from the ego to the higher self in understanding does so through right action. We call it *dharma*.

Wisdom of the Heart, **Book 1, Wisdom Note 17**

Four Zoas

Zoas. *ZOH-ahz* The four Zoas (laws) of Eckankar for the Mahdis, the initiate of the Fifth Circle, are (1) The Mahdis shall not use alcohol, tobacco, or drugs; gamble; or be gluttonous in any way. No Mahdis shall be existent on the animal level. He is a leader, and he must fix his attention above the psychology of the brute. (2) The Mahdis shall not speak with tongue of vanity or deceit or unhappiness, criticize the actions of others, blame others for wrongdoings, quarrel, fight, or inflict injury. He shall at all times be respectful and courteous to his fellowman and show great compassion and happiness. (3) The Mahdis shall have humility, love, and freedom from all bonds of creeds. He shall be free from the laws of karma which snare him with boastfulness and vanity. He shall have love for all people and all creatures of the Sugmad. (4) The Mahdis must preach the message of ECK at all times, and prove to the world that he is an example of purity and happiness. He must show that the disciple in the human body must have a Master in the human body.

A Cosmic Sea of Words: The ECKANKAR Lexicon

He shall at all times be respectful and courteous to his fellowman and show great compassion and happiness.

If the chela came to the Mahanta, the Living ECK Master and said that the spiritual contemplation of ECK did not appeal to his temperament, he would be given counsel to frequently associate with those who have gained the stature of the Mahdis, the initiates of the Fifth Circle. These are the ones who have had real spiritual experiences. Constant contact with them will assist him to bring out his latent spirituality. The Mahdis are the higher ones who turn the minds and wills of the chelas toward divine objects. Above all, they stimulate an intense longing for the spiritual life. . . .

The four Zoas (laws) of Eckankar for the Mahdis, the initiate of the Fifth Circle, are: (1) The Mahdis shall not use alcohol, tobacco, or drugs; gamble; or be gluttonous in any way. No Mahdis shall be existent on the animal level. He is a leader, and he must fix his attention above the psychology of the brute. (2) The Mahdis shall not speak with tongue of vanity or deceit or unhappiness, criticize the actions of others, blame others for wrongdoings, quarrel, fight or inflict injury. He shall at all times be respectful and courteous to his fellowman and show great compassion and happiness. (3) The Mahdis shall have humility, love, and freedom from all bonds of creeds. He shall be free from the laws of karma which snare him with boastfulness and vanity. He shall have love for all people and all creatures of the Sugmad. (4) The Mahdis must preach the message of ECK at all times, and prove to the world that he is an example of purity and happiness. He must show that the disciple in the human body must have a Master in the human body. This is a fixed law of the Sugmad. At the time of his passing, every Living ECK Master turns over his work to the next Living ECK Master who is in the body, and he carries on until his time to translate from the human body into the other worlds. Those who translate shall continue with the ECK chelas they have initiated on earth, when those chelas have passed across the borders of death into the upper worlds. Their ECK Master meets them, and they begin their further studies under him in the heavenly worlds.

These are the four laws for the Mahdis, the initiate of the Fifth Circle. They shall be abided by and shall have the respect given to the Mahanta, for each law within itself has great authority and power. The works of Eckankar depend mainly upon the Mahdis.

The Shariyat-Ki-Sugmad, **Book Two, chap. 3**

Gratitude

Gratitude, Law of. Abundance flourishes in a grateful heart; gratitude is the secret of love.

A Cosmic Sea of Words: The ECKANKAR Lexicon

The Law of Gratitude states simply that abundance flourishes in a grateful heart.

The Living Word, **Book 1, chap. 29**

The greatest of God's laws is the Law of Divine Love: to serve life out of gratitude for the gift of life.

Letters of Light & Sound 2, **lesson 11**

We serve God and life out of gratitude. Why? For the blessings we have received.

The Secret of Love, **Mahanta Transcripts, Book 14, chap. 5**

Gratitude is the secret of love.

The Secret of Love, **Mahanta Transcripts, Book 14, chap. 9**

Gratitude is the secret of love.

If you can learn to be grateful for the things that the Holy Spirit brings to you every day, you will have gained something that many other people have not found.

The Drumbeat of Time, **Mahanta Transcripts, Book 10, chap. 4**

Acknowledgment is done through gratitude, which keeps our hearts open to ECK. When gratitude is lost, the result is spiritual poverty. . . .

Gratitude unseals fountains of creativity, because a grateful person is relaxed.

The Living Word, **Book 1, chap. 29**

There are some people who are happy under the most severe conditions and physical hardships you can imagine. They are happy even when they have no food, no shelter. Yet in our affluent society there are people who are unhappy although they can have anything they want. With every material thing in hand, they blame others for what they don't have. Probably it's because they haven't yet shown gratitude for what God has given them.

Ungrateful people can never be happy. They can never be generous because their world begins and ends within themselves. It's a totally self-centered world. To grow spiritually you have to somehow get to be a person with your attention on God, on love. Then you'll find the great things in the little things.

The window of gratitude opens to us the heavens of God.

What Is Spiritual Freedom? **Mahanta Transcripts, Book 11, chap. 3**

Life will be more rewarding when we learn the secret of gratitude. . . .

The window of gratitude opens to us the heavens of God.

The Living Word, **Book 1, chap. 29**

Love

Love, Law of. The principle which gives thought the dynamic power to correlate with its object, and, therefore, to master every adverse human experience; feeling that imparts vitality to thought; feeling is desire, and desire is love.

A Cosmic Sea of Words: The ECKANKAR Lexicon

Before you leave this life, take the trouble to learn the secret doctrine of ECK. It is the Law of Love which alone can carry you to God.

The Living Word, **Book 1, chap. 36**

It is the Law of Love which alone can carry you to God.

The law of love will bring to you the necessary materials for your spiritual growth and maturity.

Therefore, if you require love, try to realize that the only way to get love is by giving it, that the more you give the more you get, and the only way in which you can give it is to fill yourself with it until you become a magnet of love.

Simplified, the mechanics of love is this: Thought is a channel of emotions and is carried by the Law of Vibration, the same as light or electricity. It is given vitality by the emotions through the Law of Love; it takes form and expression by the Law of Growth; it is a product of Soul and hence it is divine, spiritual and creative in nature.

Dialogues with the Master, **chap. 24**

167

Since we know that we cannot love everybody equally, then we can love warmly only a certain number, but according to the law, we must give impersonal love to all.

Dialogues with the Master, chap. 3

There are many routes we can take to heaven. God has established so many different paths and means for us that there is a way for everyone, including the atheist. This sounds almost like a humorous paradox, but it's true. An atheist can be closer to God than a Bible-carrying, born-again Christian, simply because the atheist may have a better understanding of the Law of Love.

The Golden Heart, **Mahanta Transcripts, Book 4, chap. 6**

Every man must first seek to give love if he expects to receive it.

Every man must first seek to give love if he expects to receive it. He must give it under every circumstance—even though he is abused, mistreated, and given unnecessary hardships in this world.

The Shariyat-Ki-Sugmad, **Book One, chap. 7**

You must choose to love only those who will be faithful in returning a love to you, and who will not use your love for a selfish purpose. This is the use of discrimination in your love for your fellow man.

Dialogues with the Master, chap. 3

The subjective can change conditions because it is a part of the universal mind and a part must be the same as the creative power of the ECK power. This (as everything else) is governed by God Law, and this Law is the Law of Love, which is God power in creation, which automatically correlates with its objects and brings it into manifestation.

Dialogues with the Master, **chap. 19**

We blame our problems on the Kal Niranjan, which, of course, is our own base nature. To put it another way, the Kal is our indulgence run free. It is perhaps more honest to look at Kal Niranjan, the king of the negative world, as something of our own creation which has no life or energy except what we give him.

In other words, I'm pointing the finger right back at the person—which is usually ourself—who sends out the blast of energy to other people. We are responsible for all the ripples created in others by our anger, as well as the ripples they in turn pass along to the next group. The higher you go as an initiate in ECK, the greater your responsibility becomes. The Law of Love becomes very exacting.

The Golden Heart, **Mahanta Transcripts, Book 4, chap. 11**

The higher you go as an initiate in ECK, the greater your responsibility becomes. The Law of Love becomes very exacting.

Whenever I look at a child, I see a little adult. Mighty oaks from acorns grow. There's no impulse to talk down to children once you realize they are Souls returned from an older time and place. They need today's leg of their spiritual journey, too, the same as you and me.

Is Life a Random Walk? **p. 7**

The Law of Love. This is the Law of Spirit, the Light and Sound of God. You can bring It into your own life, and when you do, there will be no one who can take It from you or tell you this or that way is right for you. You are going to know for yourself from direct experience with the Light and Sound of God.

How to Find God, **Mahanta Transcripts, Book 2, chap. 11**

You find that spiritual ecstasy does not touch all. But those whom it does touch, feel love drenching all consciousness, overwhelming all being. Love is God, and love is an act of God. Memories, doubts, and fears are far away when perceived through love, dimmed by love that is in itself so absolute, so separate from logic, that nothing else matters. Death is only an incident. Tortures can be endured until one dies, but it does not matter. In the end, agony dies of its own nothingness, like irrecoverable years. Love lives forever! Pain and the past are nothing more than love's chrysalis, its shell, its seedbed, in which these necessary nothings release such real wonders, such as the comforting thrill of God's hand on one's shoulder.

The Key to ECKANKAR, **p. 26**

Knowledge can bring many things, for knowledge comes from mind expansion, but the consciousness of the heart brings love, and love brings all things.

Knowledge can bring many things, for knowledge comes from mind expansion, but the consciousness of the heart brings love, and love brings all things.

The Key to ECKANKAR, **p. 29**

Those individuals who catch the full impact of the Holy Word are never again the same, because someone who has divine love in his heart will treat others according to the high spiritual Law of Love.

The Master 4 Discourses, **lesson 8**

The ECK Masters embody the divine law of love, and through them it reaches out into all the worlds, creating a wide circle of influence.

The Easy Way Discourses, lesson 7

These ECK Masters are high in consciousness so this love comes pouring through and there is no way they can block it. They must give and give and give. They become a self-fulfilling law of love wherever they go.

The Slow Burning Love of God, Mahanta Transcripts, Book 13, chap. 8

The greatest law of all is the Law of Love. And this is the law that you're interested in to find your way back home to God.

Our Spiritual Wake-Up Calls, Mahanta Transcripts, Book 15, chap. 10

The spiritual laws are based on the Law of Love. They do not punish for the mere pleasure of inflicting pain. They do it to teach people a spiritual lesson, which is part of their entire education. A little here, a little there; a little arithmetic, a little bit of language and geography. All the aspects of a spiritual nature. So that one day Soul can become a Co-worker with God.

How to Survive Spiritually in Our Times, Mahanta Transcripts, Book 16, chap. 6

The spiritual laws are based on the Law of Love.

Everyone earns what he gets. Like it or not, that is the Law of Love.

The Law of Love helps soften the hardened heart. Often there's no harder heart than that of a victim to some facet of life. It's hard like a walnut shell. And how do you get through? Divine Spirit will. It takes strength and youth and returns weakness and old age. It takes power and trades it for weakness. It takes freedom and gives back slavery.

How does love show up?

The Window of Heaven—the ECK initiation. Your initiation carries a great responsibility, but it also gives the ability to open your heart to life around you and to all of God's creatures.

How to Survive Spiritually in Our Times, **Mahanta Transcripts, Book 16, chap. 6**

There is so much that God has to give you and me. But all these different rules and codes that we live by sometimes restrict us in the wrong way without letting us know that there is a higher law. It is the Law of Divine Love.

The Slow Burning Love of God, **Mahanta Transcripts, Book 13, chap. 7**

To get love, you must give love wherever and whenever you can, because that is the Law of Love.

To get love you must give. To get love, you must give love wherever and whenever you can, because that is the Law of Love.

The Slow Burning Love of God, **Mahanta Transcripts, Book 13, chap. 6**

The Master helps each individual find love and freedom. In a sense the Mahanta, the Living ECK Master isn't a savior at all, pursuing a futile mission of saving anyone from himself. It would violate the Law of Karma. For he respects God's Law of Love that life here is a divine gift for Soul to unfold spiritually by experience.

Wisdom of the Heart, **Book 2, Wisdom Note 29**

Higher laws, such as the Law of Love, prevail in the spiritual worlds, but down here we are in the worlds of dichotomies—lack or plenty, highs and lows, riches and poverty.

The Golden Heart, **Mahanta Transcripts, Book 4, chap. 8**

The Law of Love states: to get love, you must give love.

Letters of Light & Sound 2, **lesson 8**

All who have felt the love of God must return that love to others. It is the Law of Love. This law supports the universes, and it is the only hope of peace in your time. That peace never comes through any decree by a leader in politics or religion, for it already resides in the heart, but one must first find it.

The Easy Way Discourses, **lesson 8**

Q: *What is the spiritual purpose of life?*
A: To learn to give and to receive love.

The Mystic World, **March 1995**

Love and love alone is the key to God-Realization. All other attributes and virtues spring from divine love. It is the beginning and ending of all things.
Love is the key to God-Realization.

Wisdom from the Master on Spiritual Leadership: ECK Leader's Guide, **article 86**

Love and love alone is the key to God-Realization.

Love, after all, is the great law of life. God's love sustains all. Soul exists because God loves It, and so the Sugmad has sent the Mahanta, the Living ECK Master to help wandering Souls find their way home again.

The Master is with you, always. In all times and places. He shares your joys and sorrows; he lightens the burden of fear from life's changes. Yes, he's always here with you.

He rides on the celestial winds of God's Sound and Light, so listen and watch for him there. Find him in the secret places of the garden of your consciousness. It's holy ground.

When all others fail and tremble as the trials of living become too great for their faith, you know and see the promise of God's ever-present love. The Mahanta is here with you, in all times and places. His dear presence is the source of a chela's hopes and dreams, and yes, even of courage.

All is as it must be in God's house. All is right, all is true, for all therein is love's embrace.

All is as it must be in God's house. All is right, all is true, for all therein is love's embrace.

Divine love and justice are yours to receive and give. Hold up your golden cup to heaven. Say, "Lord of All, fill it with Thine holy love and let me drink till I can drink no more."

Ah, sweet love of life. Sweet, gentle, pure, and kind. It gives life to all whom you meet, for they can feel the divine goodness in you. You and they are kin, sons and daughters of the Supreme One, equal and equally loved in the eyes of God.

Are these the dreams of a dreamer? Oh surely, the Dreamer of Life.

You share in the divine dream. You, a Co-worker with the Mahanta, help bring love and justice to all within your sphere.

Yes, I am always with you. Always. Look and listen for my Light and Voice. In them are the love and guidance you seek for making your own way back home to the Ocean of Love and Mercy.

Wisdom from the Master on Spiritual Leadership: ECK Leader's Guide, article 87

The basic law is the Law of Love. That is the single law. But some people think that obeying the Law of Love means that what is yours is mine and what is mine is mine.

Some people just don't understand the difference between selfish love and divine love. There have been Higher Initiates who have had a strong reaction to Maybury's two laws. They feel I'm getting into the social message. They don't understand the spiritual laws that govern life, and the responsibility of Soul to align Itself with the Law of ECK, which is the Law of Love.

Wisdom from the Master on Spiritual Leadership:
ECK Leader's Guide, **article 63**

In the lower worlds, the Law of Love breaks out into the two streams of right and wrong. To live here and conduct yourself, you have to know what the laws are. And if you break them, then you create karma. People can create so much karma that they can slip backward in their initiations.

Wisdom from the Master on Spiritual Leadership:
ECK Leader's Guide, **article 43**

One word of love is worth more than a thousand clever speeches.

Wisdom from the Master on Spiritual Leadership:
ECK Leader's Guide, **article 29**

To serve is an expression of divine love.

Wisdom from the Master on Spiritual Leadership:
ECK Leader's Guide, **article 5**

The secret of all time is that we are each to be a steward of divine love.

Wisdom from the Master on Spiritual Leadership:
ECK Leader's Guide, **article 29**

The secret of all time is that we are each to be a steward of divine love.

Love is the only way to God. The only way. If you want to go this route, ask the Mahanta in contemplation to be shown the way.

A Modern Prophet Answers Your Key Questions about Life, chap. 2

So what is the reason for living?

Life is God's blessing to each Soul (you) to learn how to give *and* receive love. That's what's going on behind the scenes in this great laboratory of life.

The Holy Fire of ECK, Book 2, article 34

Life is God's blessing to each Soul (you) to learn how to give and receive love.

Maybury's Two Laws

Maybury's Two Laws. (1) Do all you have agreed to do, and (2) do not encroach on other persons or their property. These laws appear in Richard Maybury's *Whatever Happened to Justice?*

A Cosmic Sea of Words: The ECKANKAR Lexicon

Do all you have agreed to do, and do not encroach on other persons or their property.

Richard Maybury, author of *Whatever Happened to Justice?* (Bluestocking Press, P.O. Box 2030, Dept. DS, Shingle Springs, CA 95682-2030) has searched the world over for [basic laws]. The laws that ethical people of all religions and philosophies can agree to and support are only two in number. These laws, already given in other ECK writings and talks, are so important for your unfoldment that they bear repeating. . . . Learn each word by heart, because knowing and using these two laws as a guiding principle in your daily life will avoid a lot of extra, unnecessary karma. These two laws belong to the social order. However, used in company with the ECK writings and the spiritual exercises, you will see yourself grow in confidence, strength, and self-direction.

Letters of Light & Sound 2, **lesson 11**

I've mentioned Richard Maybury's *Whatever Happened to Justice?* This book is for your own spiritual unfoldment, to help you gain an insight into how the spiritual laws of ECK work out here, in everyday life.

Wisdom of the Heart, **Book 2, article 13**

In terms of society the two laws outlined by Richard Maybury highlight the best of all religious and moral laws. Upon their return, society enters a new level of enlightenment. Justice comes forth to unseat many of the misguided laws.

To repeat the two laws: (1) Do all you have agreed to do, and (2) do not encroach on other persons or their property. They're as close as a whole society can get to the Law of Divine Love.

Wisdom of the Heart, **Book 2, article 33**

Working with these two laws will help you understand how to live the Law of Cause and Effect in your daily life.

Working with these two laws will help you understand how to live the Law of Cause and Effect in your daily life. If you ever have questions, go to the inner. Ask the inner part of myself, the Mahanta: "I understand the law, but in this situation, am I doing it right?" I give you this information for spiritual reasons: so you can know how to guide your spiritual life when I'm not there standing next to you saying, "This is right action. This is wrong action."

Wisdom of the Heart, **Book 2, article 9**

Maybury's two laws are the clearest example of how to live cause and effect that I can give you: (1) Do all you have agreed to do, and (2) do not encroach on other persons or their property.

Wisdom of the Heart, **Book 2, Wisdom Note 7**

Noninterference

Noninterference, Law of. Soul's responsibility not to interfere in the affairs of another Soul, but to allow others their freedom. To interfere usually involves a lack of love. Impatience and offering uninvited advice are often symptoms. Even the Living ECK Master does not enter into someone's personal affairs without definite permission. This spiritual law forbids it.

A Cosmic Sea of Words: The ECKANKAR Lexicon

Even the Living ECK Master does not enter into somebody's personal affairs without definite permission. The spiritual law forbids it.

The Wind of Change, **chap. 31**

The lesson: a spiritual being cannot violate the personal space of others, even if he is desperate to make a living.

Autobiography of a Modern Prophet, **chap. 28**

Anyone who uses any means of change or influence on another's mind, including prayer, is violating a law of spiritual consciousness.

ECKANKAR—The Key to Secret Worlds, **chap. 12**

Anyone who uses any means of change or influence on another's mind, including prayer, is violating a law of spiritual consciousness.

When we see another person with problems and troubles, we can have compassion; but we understand that somewhere down the path these problems have come to him by his own efforts. We let him have the freedom to have his troubles. If he asks for help or compassion in one sense or another, we can give it, but we certainly do not interfere with another person's problem and take it on ourselves by saying, I'm going to pray for his healing. We learn the laws of Spirit.

How to Find God, **Mahanta Transcripts,
Book 2, chap. 4**

The Living ECK Master will never interfere in your life at any time, because your state of consciousness is like your home—it's a violation of the spiritual law for anyone to walk in without your permission. The troubles we have are of our own making, through our own ignorance of these spiritual laws. These laws are at work whether or not we are conscious of how they work.

How to Find God, **Mahanta Transcripts,
Book 2, chap. 5**

"Do unto others as you would first have them do unto you" really means if I don't want people meddling in my life without permission, then I ought to extend that same privilege to others.

One is required to pay the price for breaking the spiritual laws even though it is done in ignorance. This is the highest law. "Do unto others as you would first have them do unto you" really means if I don't want people meddling in my life without permission, then I ought to extend that same privilege to others.

How to Find God, **Mahanta Transcripts,
Book 2, chap. 10**

Even in ECK we don't always realize that when we violate the Law of Noninterference, we are doing so because of a lack of love.

Stories to Help You See God in Your Life,
ECK Parables, Book 4, parable 49

People of good intentions—who are often short on patience—sometimes forget the Law of Noninterference.

We Come as Eagles, **Mahanta Transcripts, Book 9, chap. 8**

Most people develop health problems as they get on in years and the body begins to run down. That's a natural part of living. But those who interfere with others, without knowing the laws of Divine Spirit, take on more than is necessary.

The Drumbeat of Time, **Mahanta Transcripts, Book 10, chap. 6**

Whether it's knowledge of lawn care or knowledge of spiritual laws or spiritual beliefs or anything else, we don't have a right to push our beliefs upon anyone else. Nor does anyone else have the right to push their beliefs on us. This is part of the freedom of Soul. . . .

Why should any one religion try to suppress another simply because they feel it's their right to do so? This is a violation of spiritual law. You cannot force others to do your will and call it God's will.

The Secret of Love, **Mahanta Transcripts, Book 14, chap. 2**

One of the rules of the spiritual world is that you cannot take away someone else's freedom and expect to have freedom for yourself.

Some people would call this a selfish motive; you want to give others freedom so that you can have it for yourself. Well, yes. That's how it is. Because the Book of Rules, or the spiritual law, is very exacting. The spiritual laws are based on the Law of Love.

How to Survive Spiritually in Our Times, **Mahanta Transcripts, Book 16, chap. 6**

One of the rules of the spiritual world is that you cannot take away someone else's freedom and expect to have freedom for yourself.

So many people who pass themselves off as disciples of love today do not understand that simple relationship—that my freedom ends where yours begins. And vice versa.

There is a spiritual law that says you cannot ask ECK Masters to interfere in other people's lives.

The Secret of Love, **Mahanta Transcripts,**
Book 14, chap. 6

One of the blessings, and perhaps curses, of this world is that Soul can do what It wants to. It has free will.

Of course, there's a saying that my freedom ends where yours begins. And your freedom ends where mine begins. If people understand love correctly, they will understand that.

So many people who pass themselves off as disciples of love today do not understand that simple relationship—that my freedom ends where yours begins. And vice versa. That's how it works.

How to Survive Spiritually in Our Times,
Mahanta Transcripts, Book 16, chap. 15

Plenty

Plenty, Law of. We live according to the Law of Plenty when we go about life with love and thanksgiving. The viewpoint that there's enough for everybody; more than enough if people know how to find the blessings of God.

A Cosmic Sea of Words: The ECKANKAR Lexicon

This viewpoint says that there's enough for everybody. This is the creation of plenty. There is more than enough if people just know how to find the blessings of God.

What Is Spiritual Freedom? **Mahanta Transcripts, Book 11, chap. 5**

This person had a good perspective on the Law of Plenty. He felt he was rich because he had a loving mate, loving children, and a good home. He was rich in a way that probably no one else on earth would understand. Sometimes people who consider themselves rich don't have a home but they have friends. They say, "I am happy here, and I am growing spiritually." I think these are the people who are living according to the Law of Plenty.

They have found the richness of the Holy Spirit within them. And because they have, they are the ones who go out into the world and give much more than wealth to the people they meet every day.

What Is Spiritual Freedom? **Mahanta Transcripts, Book 11, chap. 5**

If you want to bring more of the blessings of God into your life, first . . .

If you want to bring more of the blessings of God into your life, first of all sit down and determine what you would like to have in your life. You have to know that first. Then make a reasonable plan to reach it. Then remember to sing HU, the love song to God.

Go about your life with love and thanksgiving. If you can do that, I think you will find that the Law of Plenty does work. I think you will find yourself the richest of people.

What Is Spiritual Freedom? **Mahanta Transcripts, Book 11, chap. 5**

Progressive Continuation

Progressive Continuation, Law of. Soul's instinctive drive toward higher states of being.

A Cosmic Sea of Words: The ECKANKAR Lexicon

One of the principles, or laws, of ECK is that there is always one more step. There is always one more heaven.

The Book of ECK Parables, **Volume One, chap. 12**

There is always one more step. There is always one more heaven.

Even the ECK Masters find the plus element in life.

We have this mystique about masters, "the perfected ones." They're perfected at a certain level. But in the absolute sense of the word, there is always one more step to go spiritually. This applies to all the ECK Masters.

For this reason, there are ECK Masters at one level, another level, and another level, and a higher level, and so on. There are ECK Masters with different levels of responsibility. Each one is working at his or her level, wherever they feel spiritually comfortable.

The Secret of Love, **Mahanta Transcripts, Book 14, chap. 3**

Because of the plus element in ECK, even the spiritual leader of ECKANKAR is always learning.

Be the HU, **chap. 28**

185

This element of Sugmad—expanding awareness—also underlies the "plus element" of the ECK teachings. That is, there is always one more heaven. Always one more state of consciousness above the last.

Ask the Master, Book 2, chap. 12

The world of the Eckankar is an endless universe, for there is what might be called the plus element within it. You never will find its ending. It is too vast for words, too vast for feeling, and too vast for imagination.

The Far Country, chap. 2

Perfection is always one step beyond the last one, and he who has a deep wisdom of God knows this. Therefore he is always contented with what he has until the next level is ready for his unfoldment.

We never reach that state of ultimate perfection for which the mystics always long. Perfection is always one step beyond the last one, and he who has a deep wisdom of God knows this. Therefore he is always contented with what he has until the next level is ready for his unfoldment.

The Spiritual Notebook, chap. 8

There is always a plus element in the attainment of spiritual perfection. There is always another step to take, regardless of the achievement we have made already. If one should attain complete spiritual perfection then he would replace God, and this would be not only impossible and impractical, but highly preposterous.

The Spiritual Notebook, chap. 2

Silence

kamit. *KAH-mit* The Law of Silence, which means being silent about the secret teachings, personal affairs with ECK, and the personal word given in the initiations.

A Cosmic Sea of Words: The ECKANKAR Lexicon

A spiritual law, such as the Law of Silence, may be disarmingly simple on the surface, but its scope only becomes apparent when the individual tries to practice it. This particular law means to keep silent about whatever passes between the spiritual student and the Mahanta, who is the Inner Master: unless, of course, instructed otherwise by the Master. But people tend to overlook such laws, especially if the tests are given in their own backyards.

The Living Word, **Book 1, chap. 5**

The holy ECK, or the Word, must be practiced in silence. Only those who have received the Word in initiation can be given the blessings of the Sugmad through the Mahanta. The practice of the personal secret word of each initiate shall be done vocally when alone or silently while in public. He shall practice not only the kamit, the Law of Silence, with his secret word but shall practice the silence in his own affairs with ECK, and whatever is given him in the secret teachings.

Whatever the Mahanta, the Inner Master, gives him in secret through the channels of the inward

A spiritual law, such as the Law of Silence, may be disarmingly simple on the surface, but its scope only becomes apparent when the individual tries to practice it.

self, he shall keep secret and not speak of to anyone else. He shall practice this law of silence with others who are not to be told any of the deep secrets of ECK. He will not speak about the Mahanta and their inner relationships, nor of his affairs in the works of ECKANKAR. Those who do are violating the very heart of the works and shall have to pay in some manner or other.

One may discuss the outer works of ECK with those who are interested and seeking spiritual security.

One may discuss the outer works of ECK with those who are interested and seeking spiritual security. He may discuss the outer works for those who want to learn more in order to take up ECK as a chela and follow the pure path into the heavenly world.

The Shariyat-Ki-Sugmad, Book One, chap. 9

We must work for our own spiritual unfoldment. There will be no cheerleaders applauding on the sidelines. Hardly anyone will be aware of our experiences in the Sound and Light of ECK as we obey the Law of Silence. The inner initiations may come years before the pink slip that invites us to complete the cycle of the initiation on the physical plane.

The Living Word, Book 1, chap. 37

The Law of Silence is good. It's best not to wear our troubles on our shirtsleeve where other people can look at and discuss them. The ECK Masters tell us: Forget gossip; it's something you don't need. It may seem as if they're saying they don't want us to gossip because somehow it's not upstanding, it's not spiritual—it's just that all those mental concepts don't mean a thing to us.

Journey of Soul, Mahanta Transcripts, Book 1, chap. 6

When a person wants to know about your experiences in ECK, you don't have to get into a big explanation. You can observe the Law of Silence and simply tell them: "It's not important what experiences I have, but what you have." Just give them an ECK book and say, "Try the spiritual exercises. . . . If you find they work for you, great—the path has something to offer you. If not, then maybe it's not for you. But try it for yourself."

How to Find God, **Mahanta Transcripts, Book 2, chap. 7**

Just give them an ECK book and say, "Try the spiritual exercises. . . . If you find they work for you, great—the path has something to offer you. If not, then maybe it's not for you. But try it for yourself."

The Law of Silence is one of the laws we're familiar with in ECK. It's simply this: if there's a certain truth that is very, very important for you spiritually, keep it to yourself.

This doesn't mean that you don't help people, that you don't talk to them about one thing or another. But if there is something that has come to you specially, a spiritual lesson that has come your way to teach you something about truth, as soon as you realize this, say nothing about it. Let the Holy Spirit play the scene out for you. Because then you'll get the benefit of the lesson. Otherwise, you waste it. It goes into the air just like empty words.

How to Survive Spiritually in Our Times, **Mahanta Transcripts, Book 16, chap. 2**

The ECK teachings remind us of the Law of Silence. If you attempt to put your experience into words, it can cause problems with those around you who do not believe you are speaking the truth. In their doubt, they will do everything they can to destroy it for you.

Unlocking the Puzzle Box, **Mahanta Transcripts, Book 6, chap. 11**

I cannot overemphasize the Law of Silence. Often, it is the sole determinant of who advances spiritually.

The ECK Dream 2 Discourses, **lesson 6**

Perhaps the most difficult test of the Ninth Initiation is the Law of Silence.

The Master 4 Discourses, **lesson 2**

There were times when it seemed that the Spiritual Exercises of ECK had stopped working for me. Looking back, I realize it was generally for one of two reasons: I had overstepped some spiritual law, such as the Law of Silence, or my spiritual life had entered one of its periodic quiet stages.

A Modern Prophet Answers Your Key Questions about Life, **chap. 2**

The Law of Silence is easier to learn if you're more willing to just listen to others instead of having to pummel them with your great wisdom.

The Law of Silence is a spiritual principle that draws a very fine line. If you have an experience that may help another person understand his own, then tell it in a fitting way.

Also be sure that telling your experience will really help that person. Sometimes we like to brag about our imagined superior spiritual development.

You can tell when you've said too much: Your stomach will knot up; you'll feel uncomfortable. It takes some people a long time to learn to watch their own bodies as a sensitivity meter about how their words affect others. But you can learn to do it.

The Law of Silence is easier to learn if you're more willing to just listen to others instead of having to pummel them with your great wisdom.

A Modern Prophet Answers Your Key Questions about Life, **chap. 7**

The Law of Silence means not to wear our troubles on our shirtsleeve where other people can look at them and discuss them.

The Book of ECK Parables, **Volume One, chap. 10**

In the dream state, the chela is given the conscious and unconscious reasons to comply with the Law of Silence in regard to his relationship with the Mahanta. As a rule of thumb, when his inner life seems to be going so fast that he is losing control of his balance in the outer life, he can slow down the spiritual experiences by talking them over with a mate who is sympathetic to them.

Soul Travel 2, **lesson 9**

When God whispers Its message to us, we must keep the experience of the inner planes to ourselves or suffer for it.

This is the reason for the Law of Silence: to let the seed of truth flower in us, and to prevent the world from stealing it from us before it can bloom.

The ECK Satsang Discourses, **Fourth Series, lesson 7**

The Great Ones, the Adepts of the Vairagi Order, wish to come and go freely among the initiates, but this means they must be given complete privacy and confidentiality. Thus, let it be a reminder that the Law of Silence in our inner life is necessary if we are to walk in the company of these travelers.

The ECK Satsang Discourses, **Third Series, lesson 6**

This is the reason for the Law of Silence: to let the seed of truth flower in us, and to prevent the world from stealing it from us before it can bloom.

Glossary

Words set in SMALL CAPS are defined elsewhere in this glossary.

Arahata. An experienced and qualified teacher for ECKANKAR classes.

Blue Light. How the MAHANTA often appears in the inner worlds to the CHELA or seeker.

Chela. A spiritual student.

ECK. The Life Force, the Holy Spirit, or Audible Life Current which sustains all life.

Eckankar. Religion of the Light and Sound of God. Also known as the Ancient Science of SOUL TRAVEL. A truly spiritual religion for the individual in modern times. It is the secret path to God via dreams and SOUL TRAVEL. The teachings provide a framework for anyone to explore their own spiritual experiences. Established by Paul Twitchell, the modern-day founder, in 1965.

ECK Masters. Spiritual Masters who can assist and protect people in their spiritual studies and travels. The ECK Masters are from a long line of God-Realized SOULS who know the responsibility that goes with spiritual freedom.

God-Realization. The state of God Consciousness. Complete and conscious awareness of God.

HU. The most ancient, secret name for God. The singing of the word *HU,* pronounced like the word *hue,* is considered a love song to God. It can be sung aloud or silently to oneself.

Initiation. Earned by the ECK member through spiritual unfoldment and service to God. The initiation is a private ceremony in which the individual is linked to the Sound and Light of God.

Kal Niranjan, the. The Kal; the negative power, also known as Satan or the Devil.

Lai Tsi. An ancient Chinese ECK Master.

Living ECK Master. The title of the spiritual leader of Eckankar. His duty is to lead Souls back to God. The Living ECK Master can assist spiritual students physically as the Outer Master, in the dream state as the Dream Master, and in the spiritual worlds as the Inner Master. Sri Harold Klemp became the MAHANTA, the Living ECK Master in 1981.

Mahanta. A title to describe the highest state of God Consciousness on earth, often embodied in the LIVING ECK MASTER. He is the Living Word. An expression of the Spirit of God that is always with you.

Mahdis. The Initiate of the Fifth Circle (Soul Plane); often used as a generic term for all High Initiates in ECK.

Planes. The levels of heaven, such as the Astral, Causal, Mental, Etheric, and Soul Planes.

Rebazar Tarzs. A Tibetan ECK Master known as the torchbearer of ECKANKAR in the lower worlds.

Satsang. A class in which students of ECK study a monthly lesson from ECKANKAR.

Self-Realization. SOUL recognition. The entering of Soul into the Soul Plane and there beholding Itself as pure Spirit. A state of seeing, knowing, and being.

The Shariyat-Ki-Sugmad. The sacred scriptures of ECKANKAR. The scriptures are comprised of twelve volumes in the spiritual worlds. The first two were transcribed from the inner planes by Paul Twitchell, modern-day founder of Eckankar.

Soul. The True Self. The inner, most sacred part of each person. Soul exists before birth and lives on after the death of the physical body. As a spark of God, Soul can see, know, and perceive all things. It is the creative center of Its own world.

Soul Travel. The expansion of consciousness. The ability of SOUL to transcend the physical body and travel into the spiritual worlds of God. Soul Travel is taught only by the LIVING ECK MASTER. It helps people unfold spiritually and can provide proof of the existence of God and life after death.

Sound and Light of ECK. The Holy Spirit. The two aspects through which God appears in the lower worlds. People can experience them by looking and listening within themselves and through SOUL TRAVEL.

Spiritual Exercises of ECK. The daily practice of certain techniques to get us in touch with the Light and Sound of God.

Sri. A title of spiritual respect, similar to reverend or pastor, used for those who have attained the Kingdom of God. In ECKANKAR, it is reserved for the MAHANTA, the LIVING ECK MASTER.

Sugmad. A sacred name for God. Sugmad is neither masculine nor feminine; It is the source of all life.

Temple(s) of Golden Wisdom. These Golden Wisdom Temples are spiritual temples which exist on the various PLANES—from the Physical to the Anami Lok; chelas of ECKANKAR are taken to the temples in the SOUL body to be educated in the divine knowledge; the different sections of the SHARIYAT-KI-SUGMAD, the sacred teachings of ECK, are kept at these temples.

Twitchell, Paul. An American ECK Master who brought the modern teachings of Eckankar to the world through his writings and lectures.

Vairag. Detachment.

Wah Z. The spiritual name of Sri Harold Klemp. It means the Secret Doctrine. It is his name in the spiritual worlds.

For more explanations of Eckankar terms, see *A Cosmic Sea of Words: The ECKANKAR Lexicon* by Harold Klemp.

Bibliography

Klemp, Harold. *The Art of Spiritual Dreaming.* Minneapolis: ECKANKAR, 1999.

_____ . *Ask the Master,* Book 2. 2d printing. Minneapolis: ECKANKAR, 1994.

_____ . *Autobiography of a Modern Prophet.* Minneapolis: ECKANKAR, 2000.

_____ . *Be the HU.* Minneapolis: ECKANKAR, 1992.

_____ . *The Book of ECK Parables,* Volume One. 2d printing. Minneapolis: ECKANKAR, 1986.

_____ . *The Book of ECK Parables,* Volume 2. Minneapolis: ECKANKAR, 1988.

_____ . *The Book of ECK Parables,* Volume 3. Minneapolis: ECKANKAR, 1991.

_____ . *Child in the Wilderness.* Minneapolis: ECKANKAR, 1989.

_____ . *Cloak of Consciousness,* Mahanta Transcripts, Book 5. 2d printing. Minneapolis: ECKANKAR, 1991.

_____ . *A Cosmic Sea of Words: The ECKANKAR Lexicon.* 2d printing. Minneapolis: ECKANKAR, 1998.

_____ . *The Dream Master,* Mahanta Transcripts, Book 8. 2d ed. Minneapolis: ECKANKAR, 1997.

_____ . *The Drumbeat of Time,* Mahanta Transcripts, Book 10. 2d printing. Minneapolis: ECKANKAR, 1995.

_____ . *The Easy Way Discourses.* Minneapolis: ECKANKAR, 1992, 1993.

_____ . *The ECK Dream 2 Discourses.* Minneapolis: ECKANKAR, 1989, 1990.

_____ . *The ECK Satsang Discourses,* Fourth Series. Minneapolis: ECKANKAR, 1996.

_____ . *ECK Wisdom Temples, Spiritual Cities, & Guides: A Brief History.* 2d printing. Minneapolis: ECKANKAR, 2000.

_____ . *The Eternal Dreamer,* Mahanta Transcripts, Book 7. Minneapolis: ECKANKAR, 1992.

_____ . *The Golden Heart,* Mahanta Transcripts, Book 4. 2d printing. Minneapolis: ECKANKAR, 1990.

_____ . *The Holy Fire of ECK,* Book 2. Minneapolis: ECKANKAR, 2000.

_____ . *How to Find God,* Mahanta Transcripts, Book 2. Minneapolis: ECKANKAR, 1988.

_____ . *How the Inner Master Works,* Mahanta Transcripts, Book 12. Minneapolis: ECKANKAR, 1995.

_____ . *How to Survive Spiritually in Our Times,* Mahanta Transcripts, Book 16. Minneapolis: ECKANKAR, 2001.

_____ . *Is Life a Random Walk?* Minneapolis: ECKANKAR, 2001.

_____ . *Journey of Soul,* Mahanta Transcripts, Book 1. 2d printing. Minneapolis: ECKANKAR, 1988.

_____ . *Letters of Light & Sound 1.* Minneapolis: ECKANKAR, 1991, 1992.

_____ . *Letters of Light & Sound 2.* Minneapolis: ECKANKAR, 1993, 1994.

_____ . *The Living Word,* Book 1. 3d printing. Minneapolis: ECKANKAR, 1989.

_____ . *The Living Word,* Book 2. Minneapolis: ECKANKAR, 1996.

_____ . *The Master 4 Discourses.* Minneapolis: ECKANKAR, 1994, 1995.

_____ . *The Master 3 Discourses.* Minneapolis: ECKANKAR, 1990, 1991.

_____ . *The Master 2 Discourses.* Minneapolis: ECKANKAR, 1988, 1989.

_____ . *A Modern Prophet Answers Your Key Questions about Life.* 2d printing. Minneapolis: ECKANKAR, 1998.

_____ . *The Mystic World,* vol. 27, no. 1 (March 1995).

_____ . *Our Spiritual Wake-Up Calls,* Mahanta Transcripts, Book 15. 2d printing. Minneapolis: ECKANKAR, 1997.

_____ . *The Secret of Love,* Mahanta Transcripts, Book 14. 3d printing. Minneapolis: ECKANKAR, 1996.

_____ . *The Secret Teachings,* Mahanta Transcripts, Book 3. Minneapolis: ECKANKAR, 1989.

_____ . *The Slow Burning Love of God,* Mahanta Transcripts, Book 13. 2d ed. Minneapolis: ECKANKAR, 1997.

_____ , and Twitchell, Paul. *Soul Travel 1—The Illuminated Way.* Minneapolis: ECKANKAR, 1967, 1984, 1985, 1987.

_____ . *Soul Travel 2.* Minneapolis: ECKANKAR, 1985, 1986.

_____ . *The Spiritual Exercises of ECK.* 2d ed. 3d printing. Minneapolis: ECKANKAR, 1997.

_____ . *Stories to Help You See God in Your Life,* ECK Parables, Book 4. 2d printing. Minneapolis: ECKANKAR, 1994.

_____ . *Unlocking the Puzzle Box,* Mahanta Transcripts, Book 6. Minneapolis: ECKANKAR, 1992.

_____ . *We Come as Eagles,* Mahanta Transcripts, Book 9. Minneapolis: ECKANKAR, 1994.

_____ . *What Is Spiritual Freedom?* Mahanta Transcripts, Book 11. Minneapolis: ECKANKAR, 1995.

_____ . *The Wind of Change.* 4th printing. Minneapolis: ECKANKAR, 1980.

_____ . *Wisdom from the Master on Spiritual Leadership: ECK Leader's Guide.* Minneapolis: ECKANKAR, 2001.

_____ . *Wisdom of the Heart,* Book 1. 2d printing. Minneapolis: ECKANKAR, 1992.

_____ . *Wisdom of the Heart,* Book 2. Minneapolis: ECKANKAR, 1999.

_____ . *The Wisdom Notes,* December 2000

Twitchell, Paul. *Dialogues with the Master.* Crystal: Illuminated Way Publishing, 1970. *(out of print)*

_____ . *ECKANKAR—The Key to Secret Worlds.* 2d ed., 3d printing. Minneapolis: ECKANKAR, 1969, 1987.

_____ . *The Far Country.* Crystal: Illuminated Way Publishing, 1971. *(out of print)*

_____ . *The Flute of God.* 11th printing. Minneapolis: ECKANKAR, 1969.

_____ . *The Key to ECKANKAR.* 2d ed., 4th printing. Minneapolis: ECKANKAR, 1968, 1985.

_____ . *Letters to Gail,* Volume I. 6th printing. Minneapolis: ECKANKAR, 1973. *(out of print)*

_____ . *The Shariyat-Ki-Sugmad,* Book One. 2d ed., 3d printing. Minneapolis: ECKANKAR, 1970, 1987.

_____ . *The Shariyat-Ki-Sugmad,* Book Two. 2d ed., 2d printing. Minneapolis: ECKANKAR, 1971, 1988.

_____ . *The Spiritual Notebook.* 2d ed., 4th printing. Minneapolis: ECKANKAR, 1971, 1990.

_____ . *Stranger by the River.* 3d ed., 4th printing. Minneapolis: ECKANKAR, 1970, 1987.

Twitchell, Paul, and Klemp, Harold. *The ECK Satsang Discourses,* Third Series. Minneapolis: ECKANKAR, 1971, 1984, 1985.

For Further Reading and Study

How to Survive Spiritually in Our Times, Mahanta Transcripts, Book 16
Harold Klemp

A master storyteller, Harold Klemp weaves stories, tips, and techniques into the golden fabric of his talks. They highlight the deeper truths within you, so you can apply them in your life *now*. He speaks right to Soul. It is that divine, eternal spark that you are. The survivor. Yet survival is only the starting point in your spiritual life. Harold Klemp also shows you how to gain in spiritual wealth. This book's a treasure.

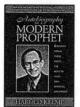

Autobiography of a Modern Prophet
Harold Klemp

Master your true destiny. Learn how this man's journey to God illuminates the way for you, too. Dare to explore the outer limits of the last great frontier, your spiritual worlds! The more you explore them, the sooner you come to discovering your true nature as an infinite, eternal spark of God. This book helps you get there! A good read.

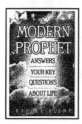

A Modern Prophet Answers Your Key Questions about Life
Harold Klemp

A pioneer of today's focus on "everyday spirituality" shows you how to experience and understand God's love in your life—anytime, anyplace. His answers to hundreds of questions help guide you to your own source of wisdom, peace, and deep inner joy.

A Cosmic Sea of Words: The ECKANKAR Lexicon
Harold Klemp

Ultimate companion for all Eckankar literature. An easy-to-use guide to over 1,700 key spiritual terms and concepts.

Available at your local bookstore. If unavailable, call (952) 380-2222. Or write: ECKANKAR, Dept. BK30, P.O. Box 27300, Minneapolis, MN 55427 U.S.A.